CU00692787

Praise for Build Your Dream Team

Great give-aways! Ideas for recruiting effectively, where to look for candidates, the idea that the company brand is not what you say or don't say it is but what your employees and more important candidates say it is when you are not there. There are really practical ideas and guidance for SMEs in 'Build Your Dream Team'. The quality and depth of the information gives the reader plenty of bang for their buck. - *Kriss Akabusi MBE, Chief Energising Officer, Manifesting Magical Moments*

What a brilliant book! As a lawyer and conflict resolver, I see the fall-out when businesses hire the wrong people. What most businesses don't know is that you need a strategy for getting and keeping the right people. Kate Russell outlines that strategy in clear easy-to-follow steps so that you too can attract the Superstars that will take your business from good to great. This book should become a classic and every business should have a copy. - *Jane Gunn, International mediator, speaker and author of 'How To Beat Bedlam In The Boardroom And Boredom In The Bedroom'*

A compelling piece showcasing measures to attract, retain and engage a successful workforce and a commendable insight into what drives an increase in performance. - *Rachel Watson, Senior Operations Manager, Tate Recruitment*

Following Kate's advice, England Squash introduced a range of objective data collection processes in its own recruitment and they work really well. This book is full of practical guidance to create an easy-to-follow roadmap to recruitment success. I highly recommend it. – *Keir Worth, CEO, England Squash*

This book is the ultimate toolkit for SMEs. It provides you with valuable practical strategies, processes and case studies to help with your recruitment, talent selection and building your dream team. Very insightful reflection when carrying out your next recruitment campaign. - *Georgina Orton, Head of Training Services, Cambridge International Examinations*

'Build Your Dream Team' is a comprehensive insight into how best to recruit the right person for the right job. It is full of practical tips and ideas to ensure that SMEs can profile themselves effectively in the market place. It emphasises the importance of having the right brand image and offering a competitive benefits and rewards package. It is written in Kate's typical robust and no-nonsense approach coupled with humour and realism. She steers the reader to navigate through the pitfalls of poor recruitment and provides the tool kit to enable SMEs to attract and recruit the best candidates. A hugely valuable and worthwhile read! - *Gaynor Cullen, HR Manager*

Kate Russell's latest book 'Build Your Dream Team - How SMEs Can Plug the Talent Gap' is a fabulous resource for SMEs, with practical advice on solving the age old problem of recruiting and retaining quality people in your business. Kate writes in a clear and entertaining style to make the subject really interesting, engaging with case studies to illustrate her advice. It's more than a legal canter though the dry and complex subject of employment law; it's an interesting and practical guide to hiring, managing and retaining the right people for your business. - *Jane Findlay, Director, FIRA Landscape Architecture*

Kate's pragmatic and no nonsense approach and advice gave me some great hints and tips on not only improving employer brand as it pertains to talent management, but also ensuring talent plans are closely aligned to the overall brand narrative. Simple, practical advice for talent and engagement managers in both HR and marketing. Great read. - *Nahal Yousefian, Leadership and Development expert, Tesco plc*

This is a refreshing reminder of the importance of powerful employer brands for SMEs. At a time where small business owners are reliant on finding and retaining the very best talent, this book is full of ideas to inspire, useful tactics to apply and guides to follow. A worthy addition to the office bookshelf. - *Austin Walters, Operations Director, WSA*

A great read with very useful tools and tips plus insights for SMEs, a well written, clear and concise masterpiece from Kate. (Keep this book on your desk!!) - *Paul Hudson, Learning & Development Manager, DipM, DipRsa, MInstLM*

A practical guide to recruitment? How about a comprehensive one! If you are looking to enhance your organisation and build a dream team this is the book to draw you a roadmap to success. - *Alex Stanton, Curriculum Developer EMEA, NACCO Materials Handling Group*

Talent is definitely hard to talk to, connect with, encourage to step forward and accept your offer! For SMEs without the big brand-mark of a Microsoft or Google, don't despair. You've got the golden ticket - a new, exciting, fast paced and ever-changing environment that's ready to excite the minds of your next hires. So if *people* are the key to your success, invest your time and efforts wisely and work ahead of time to get the best results. This book will help you achieve that. - *Kirstie Kelly, Director, Launch Pad Recruits*

A very good insight to attracting, recruiting and retaining staff for modern organisations. I work for a global engineering and manu-facturing company and it is very difficult to attract the right talent for our sites in the UK and the US. The research and case studies covered in this book provide some valuable insight into techniques used by different companies. - *Jane Ridley, Director of Global Human Resources, Murata Power Solutions*

A fantastic guide, full of ideas and examples, free from jargon and written in understandable language. A must-read for anyone responsible for recruiting staff in small to medium businesses. It addresses a real need in SMEs, with many practical tips to help you get ahead in recruiting and beat the big businesses. - *Barry Newton, Operations Manager, Deckpro*

This book is interesting *and* valuable as it gives all the right and proactive advice on how to attract, keep and nurture talent. Few companies follow through in the promise and therefore the staff turnover can be high. SMEs should treat the process of attracting, recruiting and keeping talent as a two way street and this publication will, I'm sure, be a great help. - *Carol Rhodes, HR Advisor, Fresh Direct Ltd*

This wonderful book will quickly become a valuable handbook for SMEs to assist them in finding, training, motivating and above all retaining their key staff. A business is only ever as good as its people and only as strong as its weakest link. Have you got the right people? And in the right places, with a measurable plan? Kate's book gives a refreshing reminder of how we should consider / reconsider talent strategy and remind us that SMEs are every bit as attractive to work for as a 'big name'. However the employer must invest time to create a suitable employment brand and to reinforce positively what the brand stands for and to communicate this consistently and frequently. A question often asked is: 'What happens if we invest in our staff and they leave? Perhaps more relevant is: 'What happens if we don't and they stay?' For SMEs this is a greater challenge. Read this highly enjoyable book and your staff will engage, perform and stay. *Richard Chandler, Head of Sales, HTC Health*

This book is aimed at SMEs and it does a great job of emphasising such things as projecting the right employer brand. SMEs need all of the help they can get and this great little book is easy to read and very well laid out with lots of practical tips such as '14 ways to improve your employer brand'. If you are new to recruitment or an old hand, read this helpful book and it will definitely make you feel more confident in building your dream team! I thoroughly recommend it! - *David Mulholland, Director, Mulholland Landscape Consultants Ltd*

Many SME owners gap fill without ever fully evaluating the roles and responsibilities required to deliver the products and services of a business and match skills and abilities to roles. A strategic approach is often deemed only relevant in the corporate world. 'Build Your Dream Team' is an essential guide for owners and managers of SMEs. It is written in an accessible and insightful way, encouraging the reader to consider bigger picture recruitment strategy before embarking on the actual recruitment process. The guide offers valuable advice and provokes thought about planning for and attracting the right recruits to a team. I particularly like the early focus on the strategy and actions an SME needs to consider regarding development and managing of its own employer branding, an area often overlooked but critical to get right in order to attract the best people for the business needs. - *Patricia Wilson FHEA, Senior Tutor, BA Business Management, University of Bedfordshire*

Recruiting the right staff into your team is the most important responsibility of any manager. However, CIPD studies show that more than half of UK firms do not have a formal recruitment strategy and only one in eight managers have been trained on interviewing and hiring process. With more than four in five employers struggling to attract the right talent, Kate provides this much-needed advice in 'Build Your Dream Team'. Aimed at SMEs and written in her usual no-nonsense style, Kate takes the best practice from the greatest employers and shows how implementing recruitment process in your business will pay huge dividends. - *Rob Scott, Managing Director, Aaron Wallis Sales Recruitment*

Kate Russell

Build Your Dream Team

How SMEs Can Plug the Talent Gap

Practical Ways to Source and
Recruit the Best People for your Business

© Copyright Kate Russell 2017

The rights of Kate Russell to be identified as the author of this work have been asserted by her in accordance with the Copyright, Designs and Patents Act 1998.

All rights reserved. No reproduction, copy or transmission of this publication may be made without express prior written permission of the author. No paragraph of this publication may be reproduced, copied or transmitted except with express prior written permission or in accordance with the provisions of the Copyright Act 1956 (as amended). Any person who commits any unauthorised act in relation to this publication may be liable to criminal prosecution and civil claims for damage.

Although every effort has been made to ensure the accuracy of the information contained in this book, as of the date of publication, nothing herein should be construed as giving advice. The opinions expressed herein are those of the author and not of Gibbons Williams Publishing.

ISBN 978-1-909324-09-1

Published in the UK by Gibbons Williams Publishing Ltd

Printed and bound in the UK by TJ International Ltd

Book design by Ramesh Kumar

To small business owners everywhere
Your dynamism, determination and positivity is inspirational

Thank You

Producing a book is a team effort and as a project 'Build Your Dream Team' worked remarkably smoothly because we had the right team members. I have thoroughly enjoyed writing this book and creating the finished product with the help, input and support of the following people.

Kirstie Kelly, Paul Hudson and Alex Stanton for feedback, ideas and suggestions.

Kirsty Taylor and David Rogers for corrections and editing.

Lauren Sibley for co-ordinating all the various elements of bringing a book to publication.

Caroline Massingham for her patience and perseverance when it came to the design.

My clients whose questions, dilemmas, experiments and mistakes inspired this book.

Laszlo Bock for permission to quote from the excellent 'Work Rules!'

Peter Williams for his encouragement and belief in the project.

Thank you all very much. You're a publishing dream team! I really appreciate your help and support.

Table of Contents

Introduction

One of the points on which successful business people agree is that getting the right people into your organisation is fundamental. The question to ask is: first who, then what?

In his book, 'Good to Great', Jim Collins compared a business to a bus and the leader as a bus driver. Collins argues that leaders must be rigorous in the selection process for getting the right new people on the bus. Invest substantial time in evaluating each candidate and make systematic use of at least three evaluation devices, for example, interviews, references, background checks and testing. When in doubt, do not bring the person on the bus. Let a seat go unfilled—taking on extra work as needed—until you have found the right person. Ensure your company does an exceptional job of retaining the right people on the bus to perpetuate your good recruitment decisions for a very long time. This is echoed by Laszlo Bock in his book 'Work Rules' which describes some of the people operations at Google.

Once you've got people on the bus, get the right people in the right seats. Ensure 100% of the key seats on the bus are filled with the right people. This doesn't mean 100% of all seats have the right people, but 100% of the key seats. If you think there might be a wrong person on the bus give him the benefit of the doubt that perhaps he is in the wrong seat. Whenever possible, give a person the chance to prove himself in a different seat, before drawing the conclusion that he is a wrong person on the bus.

The tough part for all concerned is if after having supported the person to succeed you conclude he is not in the right seat (in fact is not on the right bus), you have to think about removing that person. But that's another book!

Once you have filled your bus with the right people in the right seats, it becomes less a question of where you're headed and instead, how far you can go.

Some of the most successful businesses live by this principle, including Pret A Manger, Google, Hyatt Hotels, Deloitte and Mars.

Identifying the need to get the right person on the right seat on the bus is all very well. The reality is that finding and attracting good quality people is difficult. Many business owners say that the dearth of really good people is a significant impediment to their growth. It is reportedly the single biggest HR problem that Britain's business owners have today. I have certainly struggled with it and so have most of the businesses with which I work.

It's getting harder to find, attract and recruit the right people. The best candidates aren't responding to traditional tactics and we need to be more proactive to connect with them.

These days sales and marketing activity is not confined to bringing in new business. You must sell your business products and services to the best employee talent as well.

This book is all about helping small and medium sized enterprises (SMEs) develop ways of finding new talent, attracting it and improving processes for predicting success in the workplace.

It is **not** about legal compliance and all the traditional recruitment processes. But that's also dealt with. Go to the Further Reading and Resources section at the back of the book for details of how to download my e-book on recruiting the right person with my compliments.

I have included some of the processes we have used to help other businesses think laterally about attracting and recruiting talent, selling themselves to the best candidates and developing more efficient ways to recruit new people.

During the course of researching material for this book I have come across some really clever and creative processes used by a range of other companies. These have been included to help you find inspiration so you can create an effective recruitment process for your business and help you build your dream team.

Please note that for brevity and convenience I refer to 'he' and 'him' throughout the book when referring to a single candidate or employee. It is intended to refer to both male and female employees. No offence is intended; it is simply a less clumsy device than 'he/she' and more accurate than 'they'.

Chapter 1
Employer Branding

Every person you recruit into your organisation will be in one of the following groups.

A few will be the A team. They will be really good performers, needing little management and with the potential for development and promotion. You have to train, nurture and engage with them, but the returns on investment are substantial.

Most will be foot soldiers. They will be solid average performers. They are not superstars, but they're reliable. They don't set the world on fire but they are acceptably competent most of the time with the occasional blip downwards. It takes some work to encourage them to perform to their optimum but well-managed they will do their best. Return on investment is reasonable.

The last group is what I call the Pareto Group. You'll recall the Pareto Principle is a principle that specifies an unequal relationship between inputs and outputs. The principle states that 20% of the invested input is responsible for 80% of the results obtained. In this case the bottom performing 20% of your staff will take up 80% of your time to manage. Often they'll be poor performers and/or engage in repeated minor misconduct.

In business you are who you recruit. If you only recruit the Paretos you will lose to the competition. If you recruit the foot soldiers you will do OK but it will always be an effort. You won't fly. But if you recruit the A team you'll have what you need to make your business dreams come true.

When it comes to recruitment most employers take a non-strategic approach and do the equivalent of throwing spaghetti against the wall hoping that some of it will stick. If you do that you might recruit an A team employee if you're lucky, but you're far more likely to get foot soldiers or Paretos.

Spaghetti throwing is wasteful both in terms of time and money. If you want your business to really flourish you have to attract the best people. To attract the best people you have to leave the spaghetti in the kitchen and take a different approach, the starting point for which is to create a positive desire in prospective employees to work for your business. Put yourself in a prospective employee's shoes. Here's the million-dollar question. Setting aside a very understandable bias in favour of your own business, would **you** want to work for you?

The ability to attract and retain the best talent available is essential for any organisation. What is your employee proposition? What message are you putting out to possible recruits? Who are you targeting? Is your message consistent? The chances are that you have never even thought about these questions. Putting it another way, you wouldn't dream of wasting money trying to position your brand to people not in your target market would you? But when it comes to building their dream team many employers don't target the talent they want to attract.

Just as you seek to build a strong identifiable brand for your product or service, in today's job market part of making a connection with the right talent is having a positive 'employer brand'.

Build a Strong Employer Brand

Your employer brand is what people say and think about your business as a place to work. It's the view that employees, job seekers, and the public have of the business, from how you conduct yourself in the market, through to what they think it would be like to work for you. An effective employer brand presents your organisation as a good employer and a great place to work and can help with recruitment, retention and generally affect market perception of your company.

The employment branding process is the strategy and actions behind the employer brand, influencing internal and external perceptions, and building employee value proposition messages. It is a long-term strategy that can be tied to applicant quality and employee retention.

Good employment branding effectively communicates your organisation's values, personality and culture to create the perceptions that you want employees and prospective employees to have. It affects every touchpoint the organisation has with the employee, starting with the recruitment and on-boarding process. It extends to every aspect of employment including training and development, support networks, the development of career paths and benefits and incentives, right through to their exit from the organisation and beyond.

The UK has lagged behind the US in using employment branding as a recruitment and retention tool, though it is starting to catch up now. Some examples of UK employer brands which align strongly with corporate brand values are Avon, Fitness First and VSO.

While a great advert can attract the attention of good quality candidates, to get people to want to work for you and attract applications it must be supported by a congruent employment culture, in other words: your employment brand.

Poor branding blinds candidates to what you have to offer. It's like being in a supermarket and discovering that none of the products are labelled. All you can see are blank boxes, tins, and packets. You know what you're looking for, but can't work out what anything is. Are you picking up cat food, consommé or chickpeas? It's all too much like hard work so you leave.

This is what it's like for job seekers researching your company, when you don't have a clear employer brand. They have no way of knowing if your company is something they want to explore further. The way you market yourself as an employer to potential employees affects whether they want to work for you or not.

Having a clear message is vital. A survey carried out by US company CareerArc found that 75% of job seekers consider a company's employer brand before applying for a job with them.

Don't assume that employer branding is just for the big corporates. SMEs should make sure they are projecting the right employer brand too. Arguably the need to do so is greater than in large companies. There are some compelling reasons for doing so.

- In companies where the culture, values and personality have been strongly embedded employers are likely to benefit from higher levels of employee engagement.
- Strong employer branding can greatly increase application rates and improve the pool of talent from which to choose.
- In the recruitment market where competition for the best talent is fierce it can help make your company stand out in a crowded market.
- Companies with positive strong branding enjoy greater productivity because of the higher levels of engagement and motivation.

- Strong employer branding results in higher retention rates, contributing to retaining skills and knowledge.

Getting and keeping good quality employees is expensive so it's worth taking the time to get your employer branding right.

Developing Your Employer Brand

This may surprise you, but you already have an employer brand. As long as you have employees, candidates and customers you have an employer brand, no matter how small your business. And as long as people can form an opinion (and express it to others), you have an employer brand. It is developed by default and simply means that your organisation has a reputation as a place to work. It may not be the reputation you would want, or that accurately reflects the internal reality of working for your organisation, but there is a brand.

This book is written for small businesses whose owners tend to have little time and limited resources, so I am deliberately simplifying and shortening the processes that you can take to build your employer brand. One of the great things about smaller businesses is their dynamism. It often means you can make meaningful and profound changes very quickly and achieve results equally quickly.

What's **your** employer brand? Jot down a few words to describe it. If you struggle to define it, prospective employees probably haven't correctly understood your brand either. LinkedIn's Talent Trends survey of employed people suggest that 56% of people say a reputation as a great place to work carries the most weight when they consider a job at a company. If you are not communicating your brand clearly it means you're missing a trick.

Base your employer brand on research. Consider the following.

- What are the most attractive elements of your business to both current and potential employees as a place to work?
- What roles within the company are most critical to your success?
- What do you need to do to attract and retain the best talent in these critical areas?

- What are the typical characteristics and attributes of current employees?
- What are the current perceptions of working within the organisation?
- How are they affecting your current ability to recruit the best talent?

Find out what it is your audience wants. Ask people why they work for you. Understand what they identify with and what engages and motivates them. Talk to your current employees about what they like about working for your company and how they would sell their job to others. This can either be done as a one-off survey for a specific campaign, or as part of your ongoing employee satisfaction strategy. Coming out of this exercise you may well find you have to deal with some difficult responses. Be prepared to give some thought as to how to respond and whether it is appropriate to make changes. Keeping a finger on the pulse of what's happening in your workplace is essential.

With a clear understanding of these areas you can then define an outline of where you are now, what you would like your employer brand to be and the steps required to get there, all of which form the basis for your employer brand strategy.

Don't worry about being an SME. It's often the characteristics that come with being smaller that form a positive part of the employer brand perception and should be reflected in the candidate experience. A smaller headcount makes the business more dynamic, flexible and responsive when compared to the larger businesses. For example, SME employees often enjoy more involvement, see their ideas being adopted and achieve demonstrable results more quickly. This is a big plus.

Small is beautiful in the recruitment process too. You can engage individually with candidates for a better experience. Candidates often complain that larger organisations make them feel little more than a number (if they receive any acknowledgement at all). If you treat candidates like real people from the start it could make all the difference if they have several offers - and good people often do.

Be confident about what makes your business different. You can't appeal to everyone so focus on what will attract the people who are the right cultural fit for your business. No one size fits all. Every company and every situation is different.

Be honest in the way you represent your employer branding. Don't just say what you think people want to hear. Your existing staff won't believe it and you'll only attract and recruit the wrong person which could be very costly. Do what's right for your organisation, not just what others have done for theirs.

Make your existing people part of your story. Some of the best employer branding tactics simply communicate high levels of employee engagement. Seeing people enjoy their work can be inspiring. Why not communicate some career success stories at the same time? For example, Deloitte's @lifeatdeloitte Twitter account is managed by a new employee every week. Deloitte has taken the brave step of letting their employees share their stories, which publically reinforces the quality of the workplace. It's brave but not foolhardy. Because there's a good quality positive employer brand, it works.

Part of the employer brand story relates to benefits. Understand what matters to the people you want to employ and reflect their needs in the package. Not everyone is motivated by money. SMEs often can't compete on salary so being flexible and innovative with benefits can be highly appealing. Employers that help create harmony between work and home are magnets for top talent. See chapter three for discussion of the benefits that appeal to 21st century workers and a list of some great ideas that cost nothing or very little to offer.

Remember that your employer brand can't be forced onto employees. That means true employee engagement only happens if the brand is embedded into the culture of the organisation, lived and breathed by everyone and underpinned by a leadership team that leads by example. If it's clear the management team don't believe in the brand values, even the very best internal communication campaigns won't be able to instil a change in culture throughout the company.

Align your Employer and External Brand

Both your employer and external brand must be closely aligned in order to present your organisation consistently and effectively. If there is a discrepancy between how you present yourself to the outside world and how your employees view the company and what it is actually like to work there, your brand will have a confusing message and will fail to engage both external and internal stakeholders. Remember your employees can either be your organisation's strongest brand ambassadors, or your biggest critics.

Whilst your employer brand will focus on engagement with potential and existing employees, it's important to remember that most relationships between employees and the brand can actually start even before the recruitment process begins. You don't have to be a big business to be a great place to work. If you invest in your employer brand you will build an environment where happy and engaged employees spread the word, build reputation and help lower recruitment and retention costs in the process.

Once you have the attributes of your target market you can define your brand in your recruitment activity. Here are the key elements to consider.

- Describe the culture and rewards.
- Show what success in the organisation looks like.
- Introduce current employees.
- Promote awards and accreditations such as 'Top 100 employers' or 'Investors in People'.
- Set out your commitment to corporate social responsibility and how that manifests.
- Promote your career development and training structure.
- Remember to treat all applicants with respect and courtesy. Whether they are right for the role or not, they have invested time and interest in your brand and are potential brand advocates and their opinions should not be disregarded.
- Show your personality. Quite often companies build creative and innovative product brands but are conservative in their recruitment brand. It's essential to make sure the personality of the business and the personality of the work environment are congruent. Brand your reception, canteens, workstations, meeting rooms and other communal areas to create a consistent brand message.
- Be consistent with your message across all social and recruitment channels. Don't confuse candidates with mixed messages and visuals. Consistency and frequency are the foundations of successful brand awareness.
- Make yourself available. The internet provides candidates with considerable access to the employees within your organisation, and their views about working there.
- Encourage your employees to talk about the good things you do, and if there are any negative comments or campaigns, try to approach them in a rational way. Remember that what goes

on the internet is available for everyone to see, and that failure to acknowledge an issue could make you look dubious.
- Don't just leave creating and/or promoting your employer brand to HR. Everyone in the organisation is responsible for your employer brand, particularly your senior management team.

The benefits of investing in your employer brand can be realised in financial, time and reputational improvements so there is a strong business case for implementing as many of the above tips as you can. If you combine building a strong employer brand with active sourcing of talent, described further in chapter two, your recruitment will benefit in a number of ways.

- Reduced cost per appointment, brought about by better responses to recruitment adverts reducing the need to re-advertise, along with less dependency on recruitment consultants (as candidates will be better aware and apply directly).
- Reduced time per appointment. An attractive employer brand will help your adverts enjoy a better and quicker response, plus you'll find the candidates you want in less time.
- You'll get more speculative applications - candidates see and hear what you are doing, what it's like to work with you - and they come to you. That's great for your talent bank and reduces your cost per hire too.
- Employee brand advocacy. Engaged employees are proud of where they work, they tell their friends, their social networks – then they become ambassadors for your organisation and that's good for your reputation, bringing many of the above benefits.

You don't have to be a big business to be a great place to work. If you invest in your employer brand it will only be a matter of time before your employees are your best ambassadors.

Collect and measure data about your current recruitment processes to establish how effective they are. If you can, work out your current cost per appointment, the number of days taken to fill a job, effectiveness of recruitment channels and numbers of speculative applications so you'll be able to measure progress as you develop your employer brand.

Monitor your Employer Brand

Once you've done all the work of creating your employer brand, keep it fresh. Reinforce it and remind employees of the qualities that first attracted them to your business. Deliver on the brand promises you have made to those employees, whether through reward and recognition, training and development or a clearly defined career path. Your reputation as an employer is built on perceptions that are matched by the actual experience of engaging with the brand.

Your employer brand will continue to grow and develop over time. Recognise the changing needs of your workforce and shifts in perceptions, and adapt accordingly. Employee satisfaction surveys, employee workshops and exit interviews can all provide invaluable insights.

Case Study Employer Branding: L'Oréal

L'Oréal is one of the 50 most followed employers on LinkedIn. That's important because 70% of page followers on LinkedIn are interested in a job opportunity with that company. The company follows one simple principle: to attract the right quality candidates. They serve the right content, to the right audience, at the right time.

A good example was its 2013 'Are you IN?' campaign to engage followers in a fun and career-oriented conversation. The centrepiece of the campaign was a website where LinkedIn followers could go and select their 'IN' factor (INternational, INnovative, INvolved, INfluential and so on) and show off their uniqueness, creativity and professional values.

Once their 'IN' page was up, they could share it and get recognition for what they thought is their most outstanding professional 'IN' quality. This process also generated more potential interest, followers and applicants for L'Oréal. It was both clever and very successful.

14 Ways to Improve Your Employer Brand

Here are some tips on how to build and manage your company's public perception.

1. Make Sure All Employees Know the Company Elevator Pitch

"What do you do?" is one of the first questions asked upon introduction in any social setting. The "What do you do?" moment is a good opportunity for an employee to get across the employer brand. To be successful employer brand ambassadors, make sure your staff are well-versed in the company's 'elevator pitch'.

Agree an 'elevator pitch' for employees to use when asked "What do you do?" that encompasses what they do and who they are doing it for.

2. Focus on Retaining Current Employees

Nurture and retain your current employees. Make sure they're on the right seat on the bus. Proactively plan employee development and succession strategies. The more specific you can be with available opportunities, the better.

3. Promote the Stories of Your Top Employees

If you have great people with great stories, publicise them. Set aside time and money for top performing employees to talk about working in your company on social media. Let them post photos, videos, and messages to demonstrate how they live the brand. The site could be internal facing with the option to migrate certain approved content to a publicly facing career page. The dynamic content will allow candidates to experience the brand and dramatically help with search engine optimisation.

4. Live Chat Show

Allow them to host a live chat and to answer questions with prospective candidates.

5. Employees as Ambassadors

Encourage employee ambassadorship through industry communities.

6. What Are Your Employees Currently Saying?

Get a sense of how the company's brand currently is currently perceived by your existing employees. Start by asking current employees what they would tell a friend about working at the firm. Assuming you like it, package it and start communicating it. If you don't like it, go back to the employees and find out what the company would need to look like, to them, in order for them to describe your employer brand the way you want.

7. Coordinate Content and Social Media Efforts for Maximum Impact

Take an integrated and coordinated approach to leveraging social media channels. For example, if you're launching recruitment videos, have everyone in the company do it on the same day via their Facebook, Twitter, and LinkedIn accounts. This will make a big splash and get more attention versus the information slowly disseminating over time.

8. Use Photos to Promote Your Brand

Photos are an amazing branding opportunity because they drive high levels of traffic and interaction. They're a social engagement powerhouse. Pinterest, Instagram and Snapchat can all help your brand by posting company products, workplace, awards, accolades and company events.

9. Update Your Company's Profiles on Social Sites

When is the last time you looked at your company's profile on all the job boards and social networks? Updating your profile page is the easiest and fastest thing you can do to improve your employer brand.

10. Optimise Your Career Page for Mobile

The most popular time to search for jobs is between 11am and 2pm on a Monday, which means they are looking for jobs at work. And since most users realise their computer use is moderated, they do those searches on their mobile phone.

11. Use Video to Show, Rather Than Tell, the Employee Story

No other medium in the world combines culture, message, and mission in a 'show, don't tell' fashion as well as video does.

- Ask some of your best employees to discuss what they love about their job.
- Invite your best customers to a meeting and talk to them about how much they love your company and why.
- Get members of the senior management team to do a weekly video highlighting employees and teams that have done something to build the company brand.

12. Build a World-Class Candidate Experience

Nothing can wreck an employment brand faster than a poor candidate experience.

13. Provide a Transparent and Imperfect View Inside Your Business

Focus on delivering relevant, valuable content to distinct talent populations that provides a real view of the business and allows candidates to work out how they can contribute to its future success.

14. Foster, Support and Reward Innovation

Encourage employees to be entrepreneurial entities. Experimenting in the workplace is one of the most rewarding experiences for employees. Just be prepared to invest in assessing and developing ideas and giving them life.

Takeaways: Chapter one – Employer Branding

- Does your employer brand say the right things about your business?
- Work with your employees to fix anything about your employer brand that you don't like.
- Make sure your employer brand message is clearly and consistently communicated internally and externally.
- Keep monitoring and refreshing your brand.

YOUR NOTES

Chapter 2
Where to Find Talent

If you know or think that you will need to recruit employees in the foreseeable future, start looking as early as you can. It can take a long time to source and recruit the right talent. Traditional job boards can produce large quantities of applications, but the quality is usually very poor. It means that business owners have to think laterally to source good candidates.

If you have the opportunity it can be very rewarding to identify candidates with potential and develop them. In this section I have gathered together a number of different ideas to help you find ways of creating and filling a talent pipeline. In today's very difficult recruitment market it is essential to keep your recruitment processes constantly switched on. If you identify and stay-in-touch with good quality people all the time, you can start to create a talent pool on which to draw.

Referrals from Personal and Professional Networks

Research amongst some of the most successful business shows that referrals are a great way of generating a flow of good quality candidates. Both you and your team can actively create a flow of referrals. More details are given in chapter five.

Career Switchers

It's becoming increasingly common to change career direction. It doesn't denote flakiness. There are all sorts of perfectly good reasons why people want a change. Where career switchers are concerned, ignore the industry and look at the qualities the person possesses. Good salespeople are self-starters. Good police officers work well under pressure. Good mechanics are excellent problem solvers.

Athletes

A training in sports can create a good training ground for business. A recent graduate who regularly played a sport is often self-disciplined, motivated, great at multitasking, able to overcome adversity, appreciates the value of teamwork, especially if the play is to a high level. Those are the qualities you want your employees to have.

Military

The armed forces is probably the only organisation that puts as much or more emphasis on leadership training as it does on skills training. Armed forces leavers can offer the ability to work in really challenging conditions. They are strong team workers, with a multitude of skills, experience and knowledge and can be well worth exploring. More senior people have been trained in leadership skills and are able to make good decisions quickly and stand behind those decisions. The armed forces' Career Transition Partnership (CTP) provides a free recruitment service. Contact details are in the 'Further Reading and Resources' section.

Online Communities

An online community is a group of people with common interests who use the Internet (web sites, email, instant messaging etc.) to communicate, work together and pursue their interests. To find good staff with the right skills and/or interests find and participate in relevant user groups. Commenting on popular blogs and forums will help you build relationships with your target audience. For example, if you want to engage with HR professionals in the UK you would probably go to HR Zone which is the largest and most active independent online community for HR professionals, with over 145,000 unique users per month. HR Zone has an interactive forum where members can network, debate and share knowledge with fellow HR professionals.

Local Groups

Look for local groups related to the field you're interested in and get involved in their events and meetings. If an association has accreditations or a certification process then you will probably be able to find potential employees with the skillset needed to perform a certain level of the job.

Traditional Notice Boards

If you look round there are still plenty of physical noticeboards about. There are community noticeboards in towns and villages, shoppers' noticeboards in the big supermarkets, coffee shops, community centres, churches and various other places. It's usually free or very cheap to place an advert. In addition many local shops and laundrettes will carry flyers or post cards for you. The key to success is to have an easy, obvious way for people to apply for the job on their mobile device.

Apprentices

Apprentices are aged 16 or over and combine working with studying for a work-based qualification - from GCSEs or equivalent up to degree level. Apprenticeships can last from one to four years, depending on the level of qualification the apprentice is studying for. You may be able to get some funding to employ an apprentice if you're in England.

You will need to select your apprentice carefully. Under 18s are legally and physiologically deemed to be children and therefore need to be carefully supported in the workplace. Research suggests that successful apprentices in good schemes are working exceptionally well for employers.

Local Colleges

These should and can be a source of good quality candidates, though unfortunately many graduates and students disappoint. Despite this, it is definitely worth building relationships with them. Be prepared to put some effort in and be proactive. My experience is that they have some good schemes but they're not always that good at telling you about it. Keep going back to them and ensuring you're on their radar.

Be selective about attendance at employability fairs. I'm not sure if they're not well advertised or the venue is wrong, but we've found that attendance is very variable (especially when it rains or the venue is more than 60 seconds' walk from the Student Union). Predictably, events tend to be well attended by students if free food or alcohol is involved. We prefer events where we can give a talk to a group of students. Giving a dynamic careers talk telling lots of stories and giving examples can be very appealing to students.

The National Centre for Universities and Business

The National Centre for Universities and Business (NCUB) is an independent and not-for-profit membership organisation that promotes, develops and supports university-business collaboration across the

UK. Its aim is to find practical ways of harnessing the talent being developed in our universities and the UK's strength in ground-breaking research and development for the benefit of the nation's economy. The NCUB does this by bringing together key individuals from business and universities.

Work Placements

We have found that longer term work placements (sandwich courses) are a fairly reliable way of sourcing good candidates. Find a university or college that offers a degree with work experience and talk to the course director. Build the relationship and stay in touch so that when students are starting to get their work placements organised you get a few applications. We try to take one every year. Both students and tutors are wowed by our training programme and the opportunities our students have during the year. Think of it as a six month or year-long interview. Many students don't ever think of working for small businesses. Get in front of them, plug your employer brand, the advantages of working in an SME and your great benefits (see chapters one and three respectively).

Work Experience

By work experience I mean short periods, usually one or two weeks, where a student from a local school or college will work-shadow with you. If you give really good quality work experience you'll find colleges will send you really good students. Sometimes they come back as employees.

International Internships

Another source of good quality candidates are programmes like the Erasmus programme which gives students in higher education the opportunity to take on an internship in another European country. Erasmus students are a great investment if you want some short-term help, as placements can range from three to 24 months. Erasmus students are also offered a grant, giving you more flexibility when it comes to offering a wage if you are a small company with limited financial means.

Industry-specific Job Boards

Find job boards or sites that are specific to your industry and are well-used. Because niche job boards are reduced to a specific industry, there will be a smaller applicant pool applying to the position you want. You'll find a list of UK niche boards in the 'Further Reading and Resources' section.

Put Up a Sign

If you're in an area with plenty of footfall let people know you're recruiting by hanging a sign in the window. It's free and you never know who might see it!

Ex-offenders

Some of the most forward-thinking companies in UK actively seek to recruit ex-offenders. Companies like Virgin, Timpsons, Greggs, Skanska, Sodexo, Carillion and BidVest are all supporters. Re-offending blights lives and communities, carrying personal, social and economic costs of between £9.5bn and £13bn a year. There are about 88,000 people in prison. They come in all shapes and sizes and some are unemployable. But there is growing evidence to support a sound business case for implementing a recruitment policy that includes people with convictions. John Timpson, Chairman of the

Timpson Group says: "Among the bad and the tricky are plenty that are fantastic."

When interviewing inside prison Timpsons use exactly the same standards as when recruiting on the outside. They have had so much success that they opened a training workshop in Liverpool Prison, fitted out like a Timpson shop with their own trainers going in every day teaching prisoners who wear the Timpson uniform. All trainees who pass their skill tests are offered a job on release.

Some recruits from other prisons started working in Timpson shops while still serving their sentence. This 'day release' scheme has been staggeringly successful. 90% of these ex-offenders stayed with the company for more than a year.

Social Media

Recruiting on social media can be useful but it needs to be part of a plan. This is discussed in chapter five.

That said, it's worth mentioning that local Facebook pages or Facebook pages which are read by your particular target group can be useful. One of our clients is a dental practice. The company finds that it often attracts applications for dental nurses via FB, especially pages for local mums. Since the practice trains its staff and offers part time working this works well for both parties. N.B.: The practice advertises through a variety of other routes too to avoid claims of discrimination, but the fact is for them FB brings in the most applications.

LinkedIn

LinkedIn offers a number of paid solutions for companies who do a lot of recruiting.

1. LinkedIn Recruiter.

This premium subscription is designed for large companies that are constantly searching for the best talent. Here are some of the benefits of the LinkedIn Recruiter Corporate Edition subscription.

- Unlimited access to names and full profiles of potential candidates.
- Advanced Search Features that aren't included in the free version of Advanced Search.
- Contact candidates directly using InMail.
- Up to 50 search alerts per day when targeting candidates for an open position.

2. The Jobs Network

By using the LinkedIn Job Board, you can expand your search for candidates to passive candidates using the 'Jobs You May Be Interested In' widget. Letting LinkedIn members see what other opportunities are out there in a subtle manner catches their eye so they explore the new opportunities.

3. Jobs for You Web Ads

This LinkedIn service automatically pushes your jobs to the most qualified candidates, wherever they go online. It lets you distribute your jobs to thousands of websites across the internet automatically. This is a very effective way to reach passive candidates who aren't actively searching for a new position but are open to the possibilities of changing jobs. LinkedIn uses a combination of your targeting criteria and data from a person's LinkedIn profile to display your ads to the most qualified candidates.

4. Company Pages

Every organisation needs a company page on LinkedIn where you can post company update messages, provide information about your products and services, post job openings, and view detailed analytics information about the people who have visited your company page.

An important feature of company pages is the ability for people to 'follow' your company. When someone follows your company, LinkedIn keeps him up to date on your company's job opportunities, staff changes, and new product or services posted on your company page by automatically sending your company updates to his Linke-dIn homepage. Subscribing to the Silver or Gold Level Career Page subscription provides many enhancements to your company page that will improve your recruiting experience and build a loyal following for your company. As potential candidates explore your company page to learn more about your company, they'll see your current job openings on the same screen. You also have the ability to display customised content for each visitor, based on his LinkedIn profile data.

5. Recruitment Ads

These are the large career banner ads you see in the sidebar of your LinkedIn homepage and on other pages throughout the LinkedIn website. Placing your career opportunities in front of LinkedIn members helps attract members actively pursuing new career opportunities as well as those not actively looking but open to new opportunities. LinkedIn Recruitment Ads use the same proprietary ad-targeting algorithm as other LinkedIn advertising options. This ensures your ads are shown only to the appropriate potential candidates. This ability to target your ads with precision gives you a competitive advantage when you are recruiting new employees.

Measure the Success of Your Recruitment Process

Recruitment takes up a lot of time, effort and money so it's important to measure the success of your selection campaigns. Many businesses fail to do so which means they can't learn from mistakes, refine and re-direct their efforts next time around.

Start with the source, that is, where or how you are seeking candidates. Take referrals, for example. List the numbers of candidates generated by those means. From that distil the numbers of applications or candidates who were of sufficient quality to meet your minimum criteria and get to at least the first stage of the selection process.

As well as the source, measure the average time and average cost to complete the recruitment process.

If you know precisely what worked well for you, you can recruit more efficiently and much faster in the future.

Checklist: Recruiting an Apprentice

Introduction

Each apprenticeship is a set of qualifications, known as a framework, developed by the sector skills council most relevant for the sector. A typical framework includes:

- a nationally recognised vocational qualification;
- functional skills such as team working, problem solving, literacy and numeracy, communication and working with new technology;
- a technical certificate such as a BTEC or City & Guilds (relevant to the specific apprenticeship);
- personal learning and thinking skills.

Most apprenticeship training is done at the employer's premises to learn job-specific skills in the workplace. A mentor will be appointed to support the apprentice, answer his questions, resolve problems and generally help him acclimatise to the workplace and his new role.

Off-the-job training may be delivered in the workplace or through day or block release at premises away from the working environment. The modular delivery means the apprentice achieves milestones throughout.

Most training fits into one of four levels. The level of apprenticeship will depend on the level of duties you expect the apprentice to complete.

- Higher Apprenticeships - Level 4 and above is equivalent to degree level.

- Advanced Level Apprenticeships - Level 3 is equivalent to two A levels.
- Intermediate Level Apprenticeships - Level 2 is equivalent to five A*–C GCSEs.
- Traineeships - A traineeship combines training and work experience. It also gives young people core work skills and, if they need it, English and Maths training. Traineeships typically last between six weeks and six months and are very flexible.

Build an Apprenticeship Programme to Meet Your Needs

As an employer offering an apprenticeship you must:

- employ an apprentice for a minimum of 30 hours per week;
- pay at least the national minimum wage for apprentices;
- induct the apprentice and support his on-the-job learning using skills and knowledge in the workforce;
- be involved in reviewing the progress of an apprentice.

Your business can work with training providers to create an apprenticeship programme. Think about including some or all of this content in your apprenticeship:

- on-boarding;
- on-the-job coaching and learning;
- off-the-job learning;
- online learning and support;
- workbooks;
- projects;
- mentoring and line management support;
- specific training for individuals;
- assessments.

You may wish to work with a training organisation to provide training to support the knowledge elements of the programme, review and test the progress of the apprentice and provide feedback.

If you have fewer than 250 employees, the National Apprenticeship Service has a Small Business Team specialising in meeting the needs of SMEs. They can guide you through the process of hiring an apprentice.

Funding

The Apprenticeship Grant for Employers of 16-to 24-year-olds (AGE 16 to 24) supports businesses that would not otherwise be in a position to do so, to recruit individuals aged 16 to 24 into employment through the apprenticeship programme. Eligible employers can receive up to five grants of £1,500 each in total.

To be eligible to receive the grant, you must:

- demonstrate you are not able to recruit an apprentice without the grant;
- have fewer than 50 employees in the United Kingdom;
- not have had an employee start an apprenticeship in the 12-month period before the start date of the first apprentice for whom you apply for the grant;
- understand that you do not have to wait 12 months between the first and any subsequent applications. Only one grant will be paid per employer for any particular individual;
- commit to employ your apprentice(s) for a minimum of 12 months on the apprenticeship programme or the time it takes them to complete their apprenticeship, whichever is the greater;
- confirm you are aware of and do not breach any state aid rules by receiving the grant;

- agree to pay the apprentice in line with legal minimum requirements or more.

Funding arrangements will change in May 2017.

There's some useful reference points in the 'Further Reading and Resources' section.

Case Study: Stagecoach's Award-Winning Apprenticeships

Transport operator Stagecoach is one of the UK's leading examples of what can be done to solve a recruitment problem on a big scale. Finding engineers and mechanics to service their fleet of vehicles has become increasingly difficult and Stagecoach therefore took the decision to grow its own resources. Ten years on it has delivered almost 500 bus apprenticeships. Many of these apprentices have progressed into management roles after undertaking further career progression pathways offered by the company.

The Stagecoach UK Bus apprentice scheme is widely recognised as one of the most comprehensive in the bus industry. The company runs four-year apprenticeship programmes in body / coach building and has recently started a 'mechelec' apprenticeship which is a combined mechanical and electrical engineering qualification. This approach helps develop the highly skilled employees needed to work on Stagecoach's increasingly technologically advanced vehicles.

The company makes great efforts to make sure its apprentices are trained to the highest standards in the industry.

- All the apprenticeship schemes run on a four year programme.
- The first three years are spent learning in the depot and attending a specialist training college in either Wolverhampton or Glasgow.
- At the end of the first three years, apprentices gain their Advanced Apprenticeship (or Modern Apprenticeship in Scotland) in Bus and Coach Engineering Maintenance.
- The fourth year of the programme 'Apprentice Plus' has been specially designed by Stagecoach UK Bus. It is approved and certificated by the Institute of the Motor Industry.

- During the course, the apprentices continue to develop the skills they've already learned by attending in-house courses and manufacturer's technical courses.
- They are paired with a fully trained mentor throughout to guide them through the programme.

The experiment has had its ups and downs but has delivered the quality and quantity of skilled people it needs and been a resounding success.

Takeaways: Chapter 2 Where to Find Talent

- Look proactively at all the possible sources of good quality candidates.
- Measure the success of your recruitment process.
- Investigate growing the skills and experience you need by training raw talent.

YOUR NOTES

Chapter 3 Benefits

Benefits of Working in an SME

Most people want to work in a large business (in most cases simply because they have heard of the company) so if you're an SME employer you will need to positively emphasise the advantages of being an SME to prospective candidates. Here are some sales pitches.

1. One of the big advantages of working for an SME is not being a small fish in a big sea, and therefore employees are more easily recognised for their efforts and hard work. They gain exposure to skills and projects that may have been assigned to a senior associate or manager in a bigger company. A small team means there are fewer peers vying for the same management positions. Good employees can quickly acquire more responsibilities.
2. Employees in SMEs can gain a lot of different and very useful experience quite quickly. A small business creates teams of people who work out how to get things done together and learn a great deal in the process.
3. In an SME employees are closer to the core activities of the business. It's usually easier to get a real sense of what a small business does and how each employee impacts the work.
4. Inevitably SMEs have much flatter hierarchies which means employees work more closely with the senior management team.

5. Many people who opt for a large organisation do so because they think there's more of a career structure. In fact, in SMEs there are fewer managers, more opportunities to progress and more opportunities to stretch as the business grows.

6. There tend to be far fewer office politics in small companies. The reason why so many of the wrong people succeed in large businesses is that they are politically astute, visible and hobnob with the right people. In an SME employees are far more likely to be assessed and succeed on their own merits.

7. SMEs are likely to tolerate and even prize the different qualities that people bring to the party. So often teams in large organisations are clones of the manager. Small business owners want a grittier team. Thinking differently and being different is seen as a positive trait not a threat.

8. In a small business resources can be limited, but this means that employees are often able to follow projects from start to finish. So, instead of handling a small component of a larger project as tends to happen in a big firm, employees are a part of the brainstorming, engineering and execution of a marketing campaign, product launch or other important project. This can be an amazing way to learn and venture into new territory.

9. Employees in SMEs often forge close relationships with their manager and colleagues. A smaller staff size affords managers and employees the chance to bond more easily. Many see themselves as a 'family'.

10. SMEs are usually far more dynamic than large organisations. It means that they are open to trying new things and the decision-making process is short. If an employee has a proposal, it can be tried out quickly without a lot of red tape. Big companies are like juggernauts. Each project may only play a minor role in the overall success or failure of the organisation. On top of that, processes tend to move slowly through the different levels of management in a large business. This can dilute an

individual's chance of being recognised for performing great work. In a small business, it is often completely the opposite.

11. SMEs tend to be more flexible. Small companies are less tied to policy and precedent, so they can be more flexible with remote work and in general.

12. When there is just a handful of people working at a company, every success is celebrated by the whole team.

13. SMEs encourage creativity. Because they have smaller budgets, they find creative new ways to accomplish goals.

14. Employees see the good, the bad and the ugly — all of the realities of what day-to-day life is like as a small-business owner.

15. All of the above means that employees can experiment.

Perks and Benefits

In a survey of more than 1,000 people by Glassdoor, a recruiting website, more than a third of employees say that perks and benefits are a top consideration before accepting a new job. Here are some examples of popular perks.

- The software company Huddle gives employees a £5,000 joining bonus called a 'Huddle Cuddle', as well as a gift worth £500 every year.
- TransferWise takes all staff members away on annual, all-expenses-paid company holidays.
- Airbnb offers staff employees $2,000 (about £1,600) to travel and see the world.
- Skyscanner is a website which enables people to find comparisons for flight, hotel and car hire. It has negotiated employee discounts at the local pub and beauty salon.
- The Body Shop pays staff for five volunteering days per year.
- AutoTrader UK has a wine club, giving employees discounted wine delivered to their door every month.
- Jive Software offers staff free food including Bacon Thursday and Hot Food Friday, healthy snacks, free drinks including soft drinks, beers on tap and coffee.
- Opus Professional Services has a villa in Italy that employees can use free of charge whenever they want.
- Visualsoft offers unlimited holiday time and unmonitored flexitime, allowing staff to take the time off that they need.
- CA Technologies helps parents out with an on-site Montessori daycare facility.
- Rackspace offers employees an extra day off for their birthday.
- Russell HR Consulting offers a day off in December for Christmas shopping.
- Allen & Overy provides a GP and dentist on-site.

- Pentland Brands provides an on-site swimming pool, gym, tennis court and football pitch.
- ARM Holdings offers employees a four-week sabbatical for every four years of service.
- ASOS staff benefit from a 40% discount on website purchases.
- Google provides employees with free food while they are at work, with a range of different cuisines on offer.
- Jagex, the UK's largest independent developer and publisher of online games, offers staff free bicycle repairs at the office, encouraging them to cycle to work and keep fit.
- Holiday Extras hires out a cinema every year and offers a free film showing to all employees and their families.

Ideas for Perks and Benefits

Examples of pampering perks:

- bi-weekly chair massages;
- free snack cupboards;
- weekly ice cream runs;
- free fruit and vegetables;
- sleeping rooms;
- free breakfast every day;
- all-expense-paid holiday party weekend getaways;
- sporting event tickets;
- monthly drawing for VIP parking space;
- use of a Jaguar for a year (awarded to the winner of the employee recognition award);
- paid fitness memberships;
- state-of-the-art technology;
- office decor allowance;
- continuing education or training allowance.

Community Perks

Many young professionals grew up volunteering and participating in group activities, and they don't want to give those things up now that they've entered the workforce. Employers who support community activities score highly with millennials. Examples include:

- sponsorships of employee sports teams;
- book clubs;
- knitting (and other hobby) clubs;
- paid membership fees to service and activity clubs;
- philanthropic giving programmes, including employer contribution match;
- organised volunteer efforts for the whole office;
- paid time off for volunteering;
- Halloween costume contests and random office fun;
- regular potlucks and monthly parties just to get to know each other better;
- department retreats (bowling, brewery tours, etc.)

Lifestyle Perks

Millennials tend to love the 'work hard, play hard' mentality, and they see no reason to be in the office 9-to-5, five days a week. Consider:

- flexible scheduling;
- telecommuting;
- respecting employees' lives outside work (including no texting, emailing or calling outside of work hours);
- infant-at-work policies;
- casual dress code;
- wellness programme rewards (i.e. £500 a year for maintaining a healthy lifestyle)

- reduced hours in the summer;
- flexibility to use paid holiday days off on the day of their choice;
- paid day off on birthdays;
- bike to work scheme.

Convenience Perks and Special Deals

Anything that makes life a little easier is welcomed. For instance:

- postage available for purchase;
- ability to purchase computer equipment and technology at discounted rates through employer accounts;
- discounts on travel;
- specially organised discounts at local businesses;
- errand services (dry cleaning pickup etc.);
- on-site fitness facilities;
- use of company equipment for freelancing;
- personal use of tablets and phones;
- mobile phone allowance;
- employee library of CDs, DVDs and books to swap and share.

Culture Perks

The number one reason young professionals gave for nominating their business as a Best Place to Work (or Intern) was culture. Not a seat at Covent Garden but the ethos, values and style of your business. Your employer brand, in other words. Young professionals thrive under hands-on experience that gives them a seat at the table and a voice. They want to be trusted, respected and appreciated for what they have to offer. Examples can be wide-ranging:

- freedom to be creative, take initiative and make things happen;
- direct access to company executives regardless of title;

- lunch with the CEO on the employee's birthday;
- employee feedback surveys (that actually implement suggestions);
- transparency and open communication;
- freedom to share opinion and respect for differing opinions;
- mentorship to grow and improve with a 'never stop learning' mentality;
- encouragement and feedback;
- family atmosphere that feels more like home than work;
- ability to be part of decision-making processes;
- dedication to educating employees;
- support of entrepreneurial efforts and outside projects;
- challenging and rewarding work;
- fun work environment.

A Sample of Google's Perks

Google is famous for the range of its perks and benefits. Most are given with the intention of helping employees work efficiently, encourage innovation, increase skills, motivate Google's employees, remove stress and in some cases because they feel like the right thing to do. In 'Work Rules!' Laszlo Bock explains that most of these perks don't cost Google anything.

Programme	Cost to Google	Cost to Googler	Benefits to Googlers or Google
ATMs	Free	Free	Efficiency
Bureaucracy Busters	Free	Free	Efficiency
gTalent Show	Free	Free	Community
Holiday fairs	Free	Free	Efficiency
Mobile libraries	Free	Free	Efficiency
Random Lunch	Free	Free	Community - innovation
TGIF	Free	Free	Community
Bike repair	Free	Yes	Efficiency
Car wash & oil change	Free	Yes	Efficiency
Dry cleaning	Free	Yes	Efficiency
Hair cuts & salons	Free	Yes	Efficiency
Organic grocery delivery	Free	Yes	Efficiency
Concierge	Negligible	Free	Efficiency
Culture clubs	Negligible	Free	Community
Employee resource groups	Negligible	Free	Right thing to do, community, innovation
Equality in benefits	Negligible	Free	Right thing to do
gCareer (return to work programme)	Negligible	Free	Right thing to do
Massage chairs	Negligible	Free	Efficiency
Nap pods	Negligible	Free	Efficiency

Programme	Cost to Google	Cost to Googler	Benefits to Googlers or Google
Onsite laundry machines	Negligible	Free	Efficiency
Take your child to work day	Negligible	Free	Community
Take your parent to work day	Negligible	Free	Community
Talks@Google	Negligible	Free	Innovation
Loaner electric vehicles	Modest	Free	Efficiency
Massage	Modest	Free	Efficiency
Free foods	High	Free	Community innovation
Shuttle service	High	Free	Efficiency
Subsidised child care	High	Yes	Efficiency

From 'Work Rules!' with kind permission of Laszlo Bock

Takeaways: Chapter 3 Benefits

- List and sell the benefits of working in your SME.
- Ask your team about the add-on benefits they want.
- Investigate creative ways of providing benefits at low cost.

YOUR NOTES

Chapter 4
The Ideal Employee

One of the most important elements of a marketing strategy is the development of an ideal target customer profile. An effective understanding of who makes an ideal customer allows you to build your entire business, message, product, services, sales and support around attracting and serving this narrowly defined customer group.

The same is true of your employees. It's impossible to complete any task successfully **and** efficiently if you don't clearly know what you need to achieve. The success of your business is determined by the quality of your recruitment.

Have you ever asked yourself: "What does my ideal candidate look like?" N.B.: I am not suggesting that your ideal candidate is a particular gender, age or racial type since in the vast majority of cases that would be illegal. I am asking you to focus on the package of competences that you want. The ideal candidate must be excited by your employer brand and really want to be part of it.

Competencies are clusters of related job knowledge, skills, abilities, motivations, personality traits, and other requirements necessary for successful job performance. We should be looking for evidence of these competencies when looking for the ideal candidate for a particular role.

How do we go about defining the ideal employee? The answer revolves around identifying the competencies that are critical for success in the job. This is a vital step in the recruitment process and helps you to know what you're aiming for. It guides your CV screening and interview techniques, allowing you to set boundaries to your recruitment. If you take the time to properly define your ideal candidate you know very clearly who you're trying to recruit and in doing this exercise you are far less likely to tolerate second best. It will hugely increase your chances of recruiting the right person first time.

What Does the Job Consist Of?

- Job knowledge: What on-the-job experience does the candidate need to have in order to perform the job successfully? What other experience might the ideal candidate have that indicates experience relevant to the role?
- Skills: What areas of expertise does the ideal candidate have? What qualifications or certifications, credentials or other areas of knowledge does the candidate have that are required for the job? What's the minimum skill? What's the desired skill? Are there any 'star' skills (those which could make someone particularly successful)?
- Abilities: What aptitudes or abilities will the ideal candidate have?
- Motivations: What motivates your ideal candidate? What aspects of the candidate's personality will make the candidate a good fit for your particular environment and culture?
- Personality: Does the ideal candidate display the right behaviours needed for success on the job? Does the candidate contain the qualities and characteristics needed for successful job performance? What are the essential personality traits, what are merely desirable and what are those traits best avoided?

- Other requirements: What other requirements are needed for successful job performance?

To give you an example, an ideal candidate for Russell HR Consulting looks like this.

- Job knowledge: We don't usually look for qualified HR people. I don't mind a tiny bit of HR admin knowledge, but experience has proved that people who have worked in HR for years simply don't transition into the culture of our business. Our ideal candidate has a business background and has worked in operations because he is more likely to understand the client's viewpoint.
- Skills: No special skills are required but our ideal candidate has an overwhelming willingness to learn. I like candidates who display intellectual curiosity, keep asking questions about everything, apply what they learn and enjoy learning for its own sake.
- Abilities: The ability to learn and apply quite complex material. Detail-conscious, highly organised, very conscientious.
- Motivations: We look for people who are intrinsically quality-driven. It's an overwhelming personal motivation for them and influences everything they do.
- Personality: Mental toughness, perseverance and patience, humility, able to cope with rapid change, sweetness of temper, humour.
- Other requirements: Our idea candidate is prepared to work flexibly and can drive.

Whilst building these attribute lists, ask yourself the following questions.

1. Who has performed this role previously?

Create an employee profile for your top performer. The questions you ask will vary by industry and job function, but a good basis might be:

    a. What skills did this person have when he joined the company?

These should be skills identified at his interview and first few weeks in the job. You'll use this information to build a list of required skills (the minimum acceptable to the company) and nice-to-have skills (ideal candidate) to request in the job specification.

    b. What skills did this person have when he was fully effective?

This should model your potential employee when he is working at his optimum. As you use these inputs to define your employee, the skills from point (a) will probably form a base-line of minimum requirements for the candidate, whilst the skills identified in point (b) will be the desirable characteristics.

    c. Which skills did you feel were missing but would have been useful?

These are the skills which you felt would have driven past employees towards even greater success but which you never saw, either naturally or after providing training. These would fall either into your minimum requirements or ideal requirements.

2. Has the role developed since the last time I recruited for it?

If the role has developed, the skills which you've identified from past employees at the end of their employment will need to be reflected.

3. Do I want to make any changes?

If the role hasn't changed much in recent years, are there any changes you want to make? If so, now is the time to do it. Think about what additional skills will be required, and add these to your list.

4. What sort of person will be successful?

Certain types of people thrive in certain types of role. If you're recruiting a salesperson, you want someone outgoing, resilient and with strong influencing skills. If you're recruiting an accountant you want someone with good attention to detail. Think about the job you're recruiting for and consider the type of person who'd be successful.

5. Who is working in my existing team/company?

The new recruit has to fit into the existing company culture. One of the worst things that can happen after a recruitment exercise, is that the new recruit rubs current staff up the wrong way and they leave.

Consider the personality types in your existing team: are they outgoing or studious, social or self-motivated? It's vital to find the right balance in the new employee. On the one hand, you want a balanced team where different people complement each other, whilst on the other hand you need to ensure that team members are similar enough that they are comfortable with other team members.

As you consider these areas, you'll build up a list of essential skills which you can't do without, desired skills which you'd like if you can find them, and a couple of skills which will really make the employee excel. Alongside this, you'll know what type of person you should recruit, and who to avoid.

Defining your Requirements

You must be very clear about what you want your new employee to deliver. In 'Who' Geoff Smart and Randy Street start defining their ideal candidate by using what they call a scorecard. This is composed of three parts: the job's mission, outcomes and competencies.

Mission

The mission is the summary of the job's core purpose, expressed clearly and precisely. For example a Sales Director's mission might be:

To double the company's revenue over two years by closing large profitable contracts with financial services customers. To set up a new business development sales team to win new accounts and an account management team to look after and grow existing accounts.

Outcomes

The outcomes describe what a person must accomplish in his role, ranked in order of priority.

The Sales Director's outcomes might read as follows.

1. Grow revenue from £10 million to £14 million by end of year one and to £20 million by end of year two.
    *   Increase number of national financial services customers from four in year one to eight in year two.
2. Increase margin on gross profit from 9% to 15% by end of year two.
    *   Increase margin on add-on sales from 33% to 75% of all customer orders by end of year one.
3. Optimise the sales organisation performance by end of year one.

- Recruit an A-player New Business Manager by end of year one.
- Recruit an A-player Account Manager by end of year one.
- Performance manage any under-performing sales representatives and remove non-rescuable performers by end of year one.

4. Design and roll out sales training to all client-facing employees by end of year two.

An A team member will be able to do this. The foot soldiers and Paretos won't. If you have clear outcomes you will discourage those that won't be able to do this or can't be bothered to make the effort right at the start of the process.

Competencies

Hire people, not skills. Whether a candidate is passionate about your company and what you do is often more important than whether he can type a certain speed or has experience in a specific field. Skills can be taught; attitude can't.

Here are the attributes that tend to be most important to employers, though not all will be equally important to you. I prize conscientiousness, intellectual curiosity, detail-consciousness and an ability and willingness to learn from mistakes. You might well place a higher value on other scales. The point is this: be clear what intrinsic attributes will add value to your business and seek them out in your team.

1. Ambitious

Ambitious employees are willing to go the extra mile, whether to achieve company goals or make their way up the corporate ladder. They want to progress in their career. Ambition triggers openness, creative ideas, and a go-getter attitude – all of which are good for your company. Keep in mind that an ambitious candidate should have a degree of emotional intelligence so that he does not alienate most of his colleagues in the march towards achieving his ambition.

2. Confidence

A confident employee is more willing to take risks or go for challenges that an uncertain counterpart would shy away from. You can get good outcomes from people who have faith in their abilities and talents, but make sure that there is skill and/or support to underpin the confidence.

3. Humility

Arrogance is unattractive. Look for candidates who are prepared to listen, learn and take personal responsibility for their actions.

4. Committed

A person who's willing to do more than what's required from him (even things that don't fall into his line of duty), exceeds expectations and happily accepts any task or project, however difficult it may be is a great team member. People like this don't feel they're working. They love what they do.

5. Reliable

Unreliable employees are a royal pain. People who don't follow instructions, don't attend for work on time, don't meet deadlines and so on can weaken your team. Look for people whom you can trust to do what they're supposed to do when they're supposed to do it.

6. Optimistic

Optimistic people are often useful team members because they simply see problems as a way of reaching solutions. Their positive outlook cheers other people up and energises them.

7. Cultural Fit

Finding a candidate suitable for your workplace culture is important. Employees who are not a match to the company's environment usually leave in favour of a work culture or environment that is in harmony with their beliefs and values.

8. Self-motivated

Self-motivated people don't need to be pushed to get work done. They usually work consistently and effectively.

9. Enthusiastic

Enthusiastic and energetic employees are happy to learn or try out new things to aim for greater success.

10. Hard-working

Nothing can replace the benefits of hard work for getting results.

11. Team Spirit

To do well in a team requires patience, tolerance, and good social skills. A good team will be more productive and achieve a higher standard of work. They 'throw the ball' to each other.

12. Self-managed

Every employer loves someone who just gets on with his job and doesn't need to be told or chased to do work.

13. Marketable

Being marketable means the employee should be presentable to clients. He should be someone who can represent your business in a way that conveys a good impression of it to the client.

14. Detail-oriented

It is essential to pay attention to details. Even the slightest of mistakes could create major issues. Employees who take detail seriously put in the extra effort for minor details that many others possibly take for granted. Naturally detail-conscious people, or people who have learned how to be detail-conscious, are rare. Cherish them.

15. Thoughtful

Your employees should be willing to offer new ideas and experiment with new things, which will help improve both employee and company productivity.

16. Honest

A dishonest employee is potentially a liability. Honesty and transparency improve the workplace culture and build trust.

17. Communicator

The ideal employee communicates effectively, whether speaking or writing. Inappropriate or inaccurate employee-employee communication can lead to many issues within the company and with clients as well.

18. Conscientious

Studies show that conscientiousness is the most important factor for finding and retaining employment. Arriving on time, doing thorough work and being thoughtful toward colleagues helps people regardless of their job function or workplace situation. Conscientious people tend to be well-organised, responsible, and plan ahead.

19. Intellectually Curious

Someone with a diverse range of interests will often possess intellectual curiosity. A potential employee who has this trait is likely to be eager to learn many things on the job, and will be better able to step into positions of leadership that require a more general knowledge of many topics. The ideal candidate should be someone who constantly seeks to expand his knowledge, learn more about the company and industry, and develop new skill sets.

20. Growth Mindset

A growth mindset is one where the individual knows he can develop his personal skillset. It means he is willing to do so. People with a great growth mindset see work pressure and difficulties as interesting challenges to overcome, rather than as obstacles. They take charge of their success and potential, no matter where in the business hierarchy they are.

The growth mindset is the antithesis of the fixed mindset. People with a fixed mindset hate failure and unconsciously believe that they shouldn't even try a task because they are no good at it. People with a growth mindset are determined not to let failure hold them back and work hard at their flaws in order to overcome problems. People with a growth mindset simply see failure as part of the learning process.

In chapter six I have included some questions to help you screen for your ideal employee traits more efficiently.

Takeaways: Chapter 4 The Ideal Employee

- Be absolutely clear about whom you want to recruit.
- Create an ideal employee scorecard.
- Identify competencies, skills and attributes carefully.
- Consider cultural fit to ensure that a new recruit will mesh with the existing team.

YOUR NOTES

Chapter 5 Attracting Talented Candidates

In the twenty first century you have to sell your employment opportunity to a candidate. There are five buttons to push.

1. The Position

This goes beyond just the job description and person specification. That can be tedious and bland if all you talk about are requirements, skills, and experience. If this is a good candidate, he already meets those criteria. Instead, talk about performance targets.

2. The Position's Potential for Growth

Go beyond the position in its current form and discuss what the position could be and how the position ties into the company's plans for the future. Good candidates thrive on vision, so share that vision with them.

3. The Company's Potential for Growth

Part of sharing that vision is sharing the company's potential for achieving growth within the marketplace. Good candidates want to be part of a winning business, so show them how your company already is a winner and will be in the future.

4. The Company's Culture

The candidate wants to know that the position is going to be a fit, and that includes how he will fit into the company's culture. You must be able to communicate that.

5. The Candidate's Potential for Growth

Good candidates want to know how making the leap to a new company is going to benefit them, especially with regard to the growth and overall well-being of their career.

How do you attract interest from the best candidates? Over the next few pages we look at some of the most creative and successful recruitment advertising campaigns.

When I'm looking for inspiration I have a look to see what the smartest, funniest, most creative, independent thinkers are doing. I look in books, on the internet and on YouTube. In this chapter I have gathered together some recruitment campaigns from the US, Australia, Germany and the UK that I think are clever, witty and eye-catching. Some were expensive to mount; many weren't. What all of these ideas have in common is that the companies producing the campaigns took their recruitment to the places their ideal candidates would go. As one of my business friends puts it: "If you want zebras on your team go the watering hole where the zebras hang out".

The idea is not that you copy the campaigns but that you look at them and are inspired to spin the ideas to work for your business in your industry. The ideal is to find a USP recruitment idea that attracts the right sort of people in enough numbers and discourages the others.

Examples of Creative Recruitment Campaigns

This is probably the most famous recruitment campaign of all time. Lord Kitchener's appeal to Britons was a vital piece of the army's recruiting drive. This advert was part of a poster campaign that helped to recruit one million new soldiers. The month that this poster was launched was the highest level recruitment for the army in the whole of the war.

Station X at Bletchley Park

Wartime codebreaking institute Bletchley Park ran a unique recruiting campaign during WWII. In January 1942, a series of letters to The Daily Telegraph had claimed that the paper's crossword wasn't hard enough. It could be solved in a matter of minutes, they said; so a man called WAJ Gavin, the chairman of the Eccentric Club, suggested this be put to the test. He put up a £100 prize and Arthur Watson, the paper's then editor, arranged a competition in the newsroom on Fleet Street. Five people beat the 12-minute deadline, although one, the fastest, had misspelled a word and was disqualified. The puzzle was printed in the next day's edition, 13th January, 1942, so that everyone could try their hand. Stanley Sedgewick, one of those who took part, said: "Several weeks later, I received a letter marked 'Confidential' inviting me, as a consequence of taking part in 'The Daily Telegraph Crossword Time Test', to make an appointment to see Colonel Nichols of the General Staff, who 'would very much like to see you on a matter of national importance'." Mr Sedgewick, and several others who took part that day, ended up working at Bletchley Park, breaking German military codes.

TELEGRAPH CROSSWORD 5,062
13 JANUARY 1942

Competitions

Generate enthusiasm by appealing to candidates' competitive nature. If framed correctly, these contests have the power to go viral and can lead to a huge increase in applications.

The Iron Chef

One of Las Vegas' largest casinos, the MGM Grand, used the popular Iron Chef TV programme for inspiration when looking for a new head chef for one of their Asian restaurants. Teams from each of the casino's 16 eating establishments, ranging from top chefs right down to cooks from the employee diner, were given a secret ingredient and a week to come up with a menu. They had just one hour to prepare a four course meal. The winner, a young sous chef from a 24-hour coffee shop, has increased sales at the upscale Japanese restaurant by 400%!

In addition to successfully filling the position, the contest sent a positive message to all MGM employees that performance and talent are rewarded and that there's room for growth and movement up the employment ladder.

Interns Wanted

Offer applicants the chance to win a paid internship. MasterCard receives outstanding responses to its Interns Wanted campaign. Candidates are invited to submit a creative submission profiling their idea to promote a part of MasterCard's vision – such as a cashless society – including blogs, videos, or designs. The winners get summer internships at the MasterCard office of their relevant country.

If you're looking for someone creative, particularly for a role that is likely to have a large number of applicants with low levels of distinguishable experience (for example, an intern) a creative contest can help filter through to those who really want the job and have the ability to stand out.

Recruiting Via the Stomach

You've no doubt heard the maxim that you can reach a man's heart through his stomach (and that may well be true in some cases). Gyro International, a London-based advertising agency, gave this a modern twist when it started its lunchbox recruitment campaign.

In 2010 Gyro's recruitment goal was to grow its creative department by 50%. To jumpstart recruitment, the company identified the strongest competitors in the area and did research to determine the most frequented lunch spots for each competitor's employees.

Gryo contacted restaurant owners and convinced them to replace the regular sandwich bags with Gyro bags; each replacement bag included messages like "Should I stay? Should I go?" and "Is your career going somewhere?"

Soon, strong candidates employed by competitors were eating straight out of the Gyro recruitment message. The sandwich bags were distributed over one month, and within a few weeks the company had a 20% increase in web traffic and made three appointments, including a senior creative manager.

Video: Create a Window into Your World

Increasingly, companies are using video to recruit employees. Video games can identify potential employees by posing virtual challenges that require the skills necessary for a given job. This strategy also increases brand awareness. An engaging and fun game can associate your brand with positive values and company culture, and it can introduce your company to applicants who hadn't previously considered a job in your industry.

My Marriott Hotel

In order to recruit more young talent as well as attract applicants for international branches, Marriott International launched the 'My Marriott Hotel' game. Players manage a virtual hotel restaurant kitchen, purchase supplies on a budget and manage employees. The game helped Marriott generate interest in the hospitality industry, increase brand awareness and identify talent across the globe.

According to the Marriott VP of Human Resources, players from 120 different countries are running their own virtual kitchens at any given time. The game also successfully increased traffic to the company's career site – approximately one-third of users click on the 'try it for real' button on the top corner of the game, which redirects them to the company's career site.

Zendesk

Watch the Zendesk recruitment video on YouTube. It's clever. The concept is so simple and yet so packed with information and originality. The video takes a 360-degree view of the company to give the audience a realistic yet entertaining look at the organisation. I love its little throwaway comments like "Firewitch is an awesome fish". The video highlights some of the everyday aspects of working there, such as the door greeter, adding colour to the personality and culture of Zendesk. It really makes you want to work there. Objective achieved.

Virtual Office Tour

Deloitte's China division created a virtual office tour to attract talent and build its company brand. Players first choose a destination (Beijing, Shanghai or Hong Kong) and watch as their tickets print and board a plane. Once the gamer arrives at the virtual office, he can visit working areas, meeting rooms and training centres that look like those in the China offices. The game helps potential recruits learn the daily routine of a Deloitte professional. Players are even encouraged to chat with current Deloitte employees to get a better sense of the company culture and goals. Since its launch in 2010, 48,500 of those who virtually toured the China offices followed up on the company's career page.

How to Make a Recruitment Video That Attracts Millennials

Selling your business to talent by video is becoming more important. If you are planning to make a video here are some tips to help you get it right.

- Video is the preferred method of consumption for Generation Y.
- Be authentic. Millennials can spot fakes in an instant. Let viewers receive a genuine sense that people enjoy working in your company, are able to be themselves at work, and collaborate well with each other.
- Expose your culture. Millennials will choose culture over anything else.
- Millennials want to see who they'd be working alongside. The more diverse and creative the team…the better. Ditch any clip art and stock video and just use your real employees.
- Unveil the lifestyle. Millennials often choose a city before they choose a job. The Zendesk video beautifully showcased the HQ's neighbourhood in San Francisco, including the eateries, coffee shop, and bars their employees visit.
- Reveal the office. Highlight the workspace and work perks.
- Depict an actual day. Show what it looks like going to work, whom they are going to meet there, a typical desk, where they will park, how they will collaborate, and where meetings are held.
- Show off technology. Millennials like an innovative environment.
- Exhibit social perks. Millennials are looking for community as much as they are a job. Highlight community outreach, parties, and company sport teams.
- Feature your leaders. Highly visible leaders gives millennials the impression of a flatter organisation, which they prefer.

- Be quirky. No millennial dreams of working for a stuffy organisation.
- Don't create a recruiting video and post it solely on your website. Put it on YouTube where people can find it. Remember YouTube is the number two search engine.
- Our attention spans are short. Create a 60-90 second recruiting introduction video and then serve up other longer videos (if necessary) for those interested in learning more about your organisation.
- Make your music memorable. It can demonstrate your relevance, innovation, and the pace of your organisation.
- Visible call to action. Make your call to action clear and visible.
- Highlight teamwork. Millennials value team collaboration so emphasise this.

Photos Paint a Thousand Words

Insane Snapchat Skillz

A US online food delivery service, GrubHub, took to Snapchat to search for a social media intern with Insane Snapchat Skillz. The company posted a six-image photo slideshow explaining how interested candidates could apply with a snap of their best doodle. By using a platform that targets young tech-savvy talent, GrubHub's recruitment campaign allowed candidates to show their humour, creativity, and social media skills.

JvM's Trojan Horses

German advertising agency Jung von Matt wanted to recruit art directors. To find them they used Trojan horses to carry their recruitment message to art directors in other agencies. The Trojan 'horses' were 15 well-known photographers who show their work regularly to the best creative agencies. JvM integrated small job ads into their portfolios, for example as an inscription on a bus, a graffiti on a wall or embroidery on a pullover. In this way the photographers carried the company's message precisely to the target group and JvM received twice as many applications as in the previous year.

Games and Puzzles

Red 5 Studios

Red 5 Studios, a computer game company, wanted to go beyond traditional job postings and recruiting calls to recruit talent quickly. Getting the inspiration from Willy Wonka's Golden Ticket, Red 5 sent an unmarked package to 100 of the brightest game developers with a special recruitment message on an iPod from the CEO. The box also included a link to a website which was personalised for each candidate. Within a few days, 99 of the 100 employees had looked at the website and word-of-mouth about the campaign spread like wildfire. Red 5 successfully incorporated exclusivity and candidate flattery, all whilst leveraging a unique medium to reach the candidates they had their eye on.

Reveal Yourself (You're Worth It!)

L'Oréal's award winning recruitment game, Reveal, gives prospective applicants the chance to try working life virtually in several different departments. Applicants might be asked their views on the chemical components of a new face cream, consulted on the psychology of soap packaging, or expected to advise on departmental budgeting.

Participants take on the role of an avatar trainee and meet people in each department who ask questions and involve them in projects, all of which are modelled on real-life scenarios. The personalised feedback at the end will advise them on which, if any, area best suits their particular skills.

At the end, they will be given feedback on their performance, and outstanding achievers will be invited to HQ for interviews.

Code Breakers

The modern-day version of Station X, GCHQ, launched an online 'treasure hunt' to find the next generation of brilliant minds who will help protect Britain against cyber-attack. The complicated puzzle was aimed primarily at candidates interested in problem-solving and computer technology, and was only solved by 1% of the 400,000 people who attempted it! The campaign was resounding success.

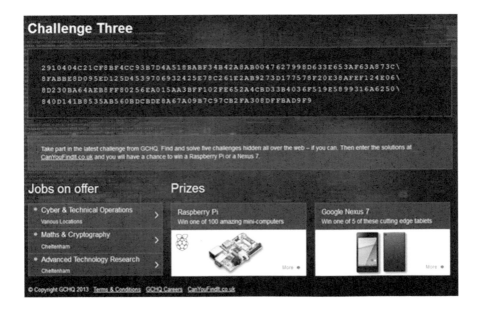

Secret Messages

Hidden job descriptions and messages help companies approach candidates in unexpected situations. They're a great way to connect if your target market is employed elsewhere, and they tend to be pretty cost-effective.

Trojan Horses - 2

Lorem Ipsum is a dummy text that graphic and product designers use when inserting a placeholder in their layouts. Jung von Matt created a Trojan horse font and hid a job ad and landing page link for a creative director behind a Lorem Ipsum text. For one week the ad was revealed when an individual copied text into his design. More than 220,000 users pasted the ad into their designs and 14,000 users clicked the website landing page. The campaign created a lot of attention in the social media and the press and reached a highly specific group of potential candidates.

Mechanics Wanted

 In need of skilled new mechanics VW distributed damaged vehicles to repair shops across Germany, concealing a job advert on the undercarriage of each. The scheme brought the company a number of talented workers and helped to establish the car manufacturer as an innovative recruiting brand.

Flat Pack Furniture Messaging

IKEA hid job descriptions inside every pack of furniture sold. The campaign cost nothing – customers literally delivered career information to themselves, and it resulted in 4,285 applications and 280 new employees. Simple, yet so effective!

Going Undercover

Companies frequently send recruiters to job fairs, colleges and networking events, but US bank, First Merit finds talent in more innovative locations. First Merit Bank recruits many people from the retail industry. Recruiters often tour retail stores and search for those with the best customer service skills. They frequently buy merchandise, testing whether the salespeople will effectively up-sell them. But the assessment doesn't stop there. The talent agents return the merchandise to test how the salesperson handles a return. Though the recruits might not have experience in banking, they're pursued because of their customer service skills, which can be applied to various industries.

This is a good example of finding relevant raw skills and transferring them to other sectors.

Appiness

Advertising giant Saatchi & Saatchi, wanted to engage advertising creatives in an unexpected way during their everyday workflow. They developed an app through which creatives could submit an idea and instantly receive feedback from the company's Mobile Creative Director.

After using the app a few times, people received a message that Saatchi & Saatchi was hiring. Not only is this game involved and targeted, but it also involved candidates in generating a dialogue with a manager that they would be working with. After launching the campaign, the agency reported that their applicant pool had nearly doubled.

Referrals

While many companies stick to the promise of monetary rewards to foster employee referrals, recent studies have found that only 11% of employees make referrals because of the opportunity to earn bonus income. In 2012, Carmax, the largest used-car retailer in the United States, needed a new way to go about powering employees for its busiest season.

Carmax encouraged its employees to wear a blue bracelet with the question, 'Who do you know?' in order to break the ice between employees and their networks. The bracelet served as a reminder for associates to invite people they believe to be a good fit to apply to Carmax, and it provided an easy conversation starter with friends and family who asked questions about the bracelet.

The company says it only employs about one out of every 35 applicants, and approximately 36% of new recruits are referred by employees.

Some companies have broadened this technique to anyone. When Studio Digita Web Design was looking for new staff its MD, Travis Bennett, ran a series of Facebook ads that mentioned the company was looking for staff, and would pay out a referral fee to anyone. They received a huge influx of recommendations from friends and friends of friends, all looking to cash in. They found a good quality team member. Travis adds that this technique also got the agency in front of a new people at the same time.

How to Encourage Referrals

Create Your Own Flow of Referrals

Ask for referrals to generate a flow of good quality candidates and create your personal pool of talent.

- Whenever you meet anyone new ask: "Who are the most talented people you know that I should recruit?" They are usually happy to give details. Call a few people from that list every week and then stay in touch with those with the most promise.
- Identify ten extremely talented people off the top of your head. Call your list and ask the question: "Who are the most talented people you know that I should bring into my business?" It can generate 50-100 names.
- Ask your customers for the names of the most talented sales people who call them.
- Ask business partners who they think are the most effective business developers.
- Ask your suppliers who are their strongest purchasing agents.
- Join professional organisations and ask the people you meet through events. When you meet new people almost the first question that people ask is "What do you do?" Tell them, then follow up with "Now that I've told you what I do, who are the most talented people you know who would be a good fit for my company?"
- Manage your referral prospects using an applicant tracking system (ATS).

Referrals from Employees

After you, your employees know your business better than anyone. Turn your team into talent spotters to source good people.

Don't wait until you've got a vacancy. Say to your team: "If you spot someone like us – it could be a customer, supplier, friends, competitor, person you meet when you're out and about, get his details and tell us. We want to talk to him."

Make in-house referrals part of your development and progression process. Try including something along the lines of "Source three A-team candidates a year" and reward them by providing a financial or other incentive.

A good employee referral programme is a recruiter's best friend. It allows you to turn your workforce into recruiters. Studies also show that referred candidates, if appointed, stay at their jobs longer than traditional recruits.

Start by ensuring your business is a good place to refer people to – see chapter one on employer branding. Have a clear view of what it should accomplish. For example, some companies that have sought to improve their diversity via referrals are looking for a select group of employees to refer more. Other companies want to increase referrals in specific areas of their company, such as sales.

Make the process easy for your team. The less work an employee has to do to refer a candidate, the more successful the programme will be. The best-case scenario is that an employee just has to provide the recruiting team with a name and some way to contact the referred candidate, and the recruiting team takes over from there.

Train your employees on how to use the referral programme. That training should cover three aspects.

1. The practical nature of how to use the system.
2. What your company is looking for in referred candidates.

3. What employees can expect when they refer a candidate.

People need to know how to use your employee referral system. Teach your employees what your company is looking for. While many of your employees might already know this, it's a good time to talk about what you value in a candidate. The aim of this is to ensure you get high-quality referrals from your employees. Because, if your employees are constantly giving you people you have no interest in, it will create both more work for you and more frustration for them.

Make clear what employees can expect when they refer a candidate. How will the candidate be contacted and when? The worst mistake a company can make with its referral programme is to not contact referred candidates when an employee expects them to. If that happens, it's unlikely that employee will refer anyone else.

What's the best way to conduct the training? It depends on the size of the company. A smaller company might be able to have a 30-minute in-person company meeting to explain it, whereas a larger company will probably have to do something digital. Either way, it should be relatively short, engaging and make both the process and the expectations clear.

One of the biggest reasons employees don't refer more candidates is they don't know what jobs the company's recruiting for. So, once you build your programme and train your workforce how to use it, it's time to put on your marketing hat and keep employees abreast of the vacancies and new opportunities.

Once your programme's set up, remind your employees about open positions and the referrals that are starting to come in. Share those benefits with the employees who are referring candidates. The most common way companies do this is through money via a referral bonus.

However, cash bonuses aren't necessary, and even if you do give them, other forms of recognition are nice as well.

No matter what you do, doing something is important. An employee who refers a candidate and gets some positive recognition is likely to refer again, and it will inspire others to do so as well.

Measure the results of your referral programme. You can do this in several ways.

1. The overall percentage of recruits who came from referrals.

The most common and most obvious statistic to measure is the percentage of new recruits who were referred by an employee. If this number isn't as high as you'd like, try to find ways to make it even easier for your employees to refer a candidate or do a better job of reminding your workforce of the open positions within your company.

2. The percentage of 'qualified' referrals.

This means the amount of referred candidates who are deemed qualified enough for an interview. This number should be (probably quite a bit) higher than the percentage of all applicants who get an interview. If it isn't, it may mean your employees are referring the wrong people. To solve this, you may need to set clear expectations and standards for what your company is looking for.

3. Your workforce's participation rate in the referral programme.

All too often, a small percentage of a company's workforce is responsible for the vast majority of its referrals. If this number is low, it often means you need to do a better job of marketing your referral programme and the open jobs within your company to your entire workforce.

The quality of referred candidates.

Research suggests employees you get from referrals are of better quality than non-referred candidates. That said, you have to measure this as well to ensure your employees are referring the right people.

Measuring quality is always tricky, but you can use numbers like a new employee's tenure at your company or how well he does in performance reviews. Again, if this statistic is poor, it's worth training your employees on what types of people to refer.

Employee referrals are one of the best ways to source candidates, as they get you better people, quicker. Simply put, a company that doesn't have a strong referral programme is one that's missing out on a great opportunity.

Guerrilla Recruiting

'Off-the-wall' campaigns that approach recruitment problems in unique ways are a great tactic if you want to go viral as they tend to be widely shared.

The 'Geek Stealers'

Faced with a shortage of Australian engineers, software company Atlassian launched a campaign to 'steal' European geeks and relocate 15 developers to Sydney. Decking out a bus and hosting meetups and interviews all over Europe, potential candidates could track the bus's progress and apply for a chance to move to Australia's 'Silicon Beach'.

This was not Atlassian's first time at the recruiting rodeo. Their 2010, 32 Campaign offered new recruits a holiday when hired to start their new job feeling happy and refreshed. Atlassian's Global Talent & Culture Chief Joris Luijke's objective? To make Atlassian the world's best workplace, and he says he and his team approach recruitment differently than other companies who use the same search tools and look in the same places. His recruiting strategies combine excellent searching, great recruitment branding, and extending their recruiting message as wide as possible.

Social Media

Deloitte in the Netherlands has around 4,600 employees. As only 10% of the workforce is looking for a new job at any one time, including people without a job, the Dutch labour market is a tough one for the employers.

In 2010/2011 Deloitte's Dutch online recruitment team had the following objectives.

- Help to fill the roles at Deloitte and reach the target of 1,000 new recruits.
- Develop a strong employer brand which attracts the right candidates for Deloitte.
- Drive traffic to their career website to create a funnel of candidates and support the employer brand.

Deloitte built a career website called Werken bij Deloitte (Work at Deloitte) which sits completely outside Deloitte's corporate website. They have made it very personal for visitors.

- The website has three categories: Students, Young Professional and Professional. Content is created specifically for each category, with different questions addressed and different content provided depending on the visitor.
- On all pages, the company has included testimonials and videos from current employees.
- Each recruiter has a profile, including a short bio.
- The recruitment team are very accessible. The website shows their direct phone numbers and email addresses and visitors can see when they are online or offline if they want to have a live chat with them.

Personal content is key to the company's recruitment strategy. They produce, manage and use content which is either produced by the team or by employees from Deloitte. The website content is integrated with social media. Deloitte engaged with employees through social media to generate both content and lively discussions. For example they looked for bloggers within Deloitte to write about what they do or how they feel. They ran contests with employees on social media, asking employees to support a new campaign for employer branding aimed at students. One example was to load a photo with the theme 'spot the green spot' (relating to Deloitte's logo where there is a green spot) using hashtag #beginneersthier. The winner needed 1,000 plus views and had to show creativity. Offering an iPhone as a prize encouraged reasonable activity and the online team posted the contest on Facebook, Twitter and communicated energetically about the competition. 55 photos were uploaded and there were 15,500 views within five weeks.

Deloitte used Google Analytics to measure where their candidates came from, how long it took and the conversion rate between traffic/applications and jobs. The Werken bij Deloitte website generates more traffic that the corporate websites with 234% more traffic coming from social media than from the other sources. The costs of recruitment via agencies dropped significantly and the investment in job boards costs steadily reduced.

Social media is still giving Deloitte great success.

- Twitter @WekbijDeloitte is used to post jobs and events and alert people to new blog posts. The strength of their Twitter presence lies in the fact that all recruiters have a Twitter account and tweet as well.
- Their Facebook page focuses on potential candidates. The company is making contact with passive candidates this way

by sharing knowledge, building a relationship and keeping them informed.

- LinkedIn is used to source experienced candidates. The recruitment team can search for professionals by looking at their network and recommendations. It also posts vacancies in the LinkedIn group.
- YouTube is used as a way to communicate their employee testimonials and these videos are embedded on the actual career website.

Using a great deal of content generated by employees which it can publish across social media channels, Deloitte created a very human story with personal bios, photos and easy ways to contact and connect with them. Although appointments made directly through social media represent only 2% of the total the indirect benefits of social media are much greater.

How to Use Social Media in Recruitment

Using social media effectively as part of recruitment is not quite as easy as sending some tweets and setting up a Facebook page. Now that most businesses try to find potential employees and customers using social media, it's much harder to stand out from the digital mass.

Who Do You Want to Attract?

Understand who you're trying to reach. Without this, you can't create a process that works. Think about which social media channels your target recruits are most likely to use. Facebook and Twitter are generally a given amongst graduates, but what kind of person are you looking for? Someone more creative might use Pinterest as a source of inspiration; someone who has a confident and engaging personality might watch and create videos on YouTube.

Ask yourself the following questions.

- What are their hobbies likely to be? How would this make them suitable for the role?
- What kind of publications or public figures are they likely to follow?
- What subjects would they have studied?
- Is there an online platform for these subjects that they are likely to engage with?
- What extra-curricular activities might they take part in?
- How are they involved with these online? This could take the form of Facebook or LinkedIn groups.

The clearer a picture you have of the person you're looking for, the easier it will be to know where he spends his time online, and therefore where you should be spending yours in order to engage with him.

Be Seen

Your social media content and activity will be worthless if nobody sees it. One of the most obvious ways to get your channel seen by more people is by gaining more followers which is easy in theory, but not quite so easy in practice. Twitter is the channel that makes this easiest for you; once you know which accounts your candidates are likely to follow, you can then start to follow your candidates in the hope that they return the favour. Tools like Manage Flitter make this process a little easier, but it still takes a lot of time to build up those numbers.

A more expensive, but often effective, way of getting your company in front of the best talent is to use paid advertisements on social media. All channels offer the opportunity to bump your post to the top of your followers' feeds, but you need to be clever about it.

When sponsoring or boosting a post, the key is the audience to whom you're actually promoting it. Most social media networks allow you to narrow down your audience by age, location, interests. The more focused you can make your target audience, the more successful your paid ads will be and the more return you will see on your investment.

Engage With Your Followers

Give your followers a reason to engage with you. Create an online community for your followers to feel a part of and get involved in. The key is giving followers the opportunity and a content creator for your feed. For example, Gradvert's Twitter session (#GradsHour) which takes place every Wednesday, allows businesses to share their current vacancies live with potential candidates.

Think about how you can increase engagement on your social media feeds. How can you get your followers to create content for you?

- Use hashtags. You can use these to start a conversation. It's an easy method, but takes commitment to see long term results.
- Launch a competition asking followers to submit their own entries and opinions. If you start talking to your followers, make sure you reward those who engage by consistently sharing and replying to their contributions.

Show You're an Excellent Employer

Being an employer of choice goes back to your employer branding. A report from Harvard Business Review states that "Today, younger people are looking for an additional form of compensation: an organisation that allows them to do meaningful work, while offering opportunities for personal growth and autonomy. ... The next generation is telling companies that to become an employer of choice, they must become social value creators."

Social media is a good medium to communicate your values and opportunities to potential candidates. Show your business at a deeper level and start sharing your core values, your vision, and your mission statement. This allows prospective employees to engage with your company in a much more personal way and will attract those who share your core values. It goes back to employer branding again.

Use original visual content like photos, infographics and videos with your followers on social media, which will allow prospective employees to see themselves working for you in a more realistic way.

The Facebook page for BP careers is a good example (https://en-gb. facebook.com/bpcareers).

Measure Progress

List the goals of your campaign. Is it the number of CVs received? The number of placements? The level of engagement?

Find ways to measure them. Actions like setting up dedicated landing pages which you can easily do using pay-as-you-go programmes like Instapage (www.instapage.com) and separate email addresses which are only shared on social media, will give you a good sense of how many leads are coming from there. Tools like Google Analytics and SumoMe are helpful for showing you the volume of traffic coming to your website from social media through measures like bounce rate, goal conversions and time spent on site.

Visual Job Adverts

Strong visual adverts can really make you stand out from the crowd. There are many clever adverts. Here are a few to set you thinking.

There are 10 mistakes in this ad.

If you beleive you're a great grafic deigner

with an eye for details, Spot these mistakes,

than sent us your feedback on the pelow address

including your   CV & portfolio

joe@horizonfcb.net

If you can decipher this, you've got the job!

"A FIN AL AVVV WON MOH BEFAW AH GO OME."

IF YOU'RE AN EXPERIENCED BARTENDER AND YOU CAN DECIPHER THIS BABBLE, WE'D LIKE TO HEAR FROM YOU.

Walk-in interviews from Monday 20th to Wednesday 22nd April from 2pm till 5pm at Dallas Restaurant & Bar, 31 Boat Quay, Singapore. Singaporean and PR only. Applicants may also apply via email at admin@dallas.sg or call 6532 2131.
(Those lacking a great sense of humour need not apply).

www.dallas.sg

McDonald's wanted to emphasise the fact
that candidates can learn and have a career.

Quirky Pictures Attract Millennials

Takeaways: Chapter 5
Attracting Talented Candidates

- Push the five interest buttons.
- Target your campaigns where your ideal candidates go.
- Take inspiration from creative recruitment campaigns.
- Consider making a recruitment video.
- Actively build a referral programme.
- Measure outcomes.

YOUR NOTES

Chapter 6 Assess Applications Efficiently

Once you have tried and tested your process for attracting talented candidates you must decide how to assess their applications. Your objectives here are to devise an efficient process that doesn't tie up too much of your time, takes applicants through the recruitment reasonably quickly (millennials dislike protracted selection processes) and is a good predictor of success. N.B.: Respond with a courteous reply to all submissions, even if you are sending a regret.

Setting up a more creative interview process requires a candidate to take the time to make the application. This means you are more likely to get applications from people who are genuinely interested. Here are some suggestions how to screen efficiently while gaining some useful data about the candidate.

1. Describe in 100 Words or Fewer ...

Ask candidates to send you their CV plus 100 words describing why they want to work for you and why they'd be good. An ability to do this shows creativity and an ability to communicate succinctly. It is also a lot more interesting than reading dull standard cover letters.

2. Video Introduction

If presentation is important to the role's success, asking for a video introduction is a useful screening activity. Provide a theme and time limit. Make it clear that the video doesn't have to be Spielberg quality. It can be shot with a smart phone or flick camera. You're interested in the candidate's content, not the special effects.

3. Work Related Case Studies

Case studies can disclose the way a candidate thinks and approaches problem solving. If the role for which you're recruiting requires an analytical brain, provide the candidate with some hypothetical case studies to tackle. He should be able to ask questions and use a calculator if necessary.

4. Job Simulation

By far the best predictor of success in a role is asking candidates to do a work-related task. For example, one car showroom business I know asks sales candidates to choose an item and come to the interview ready to sell it to the interviewer.

Ask yourself, what are the core competencies of this role that could be distilled into a 20 – to – 60 minute trial? Then design a task around them.

It's best to keep this screening technique for a later stage of the process because it's likely to take a good deal of time and preparation on behalf of the candidate.

5. Work Portfolio

Work portfolios don't have to be limited to design and photographic businesses. They can be extended to other professions that don't usually ask to see them. Events management, product management, content marketers, and landscaping are all professions that create projects which are visually represented. Ask for examples of work and see what the candidates return.

6. Let Candidates Interact with Current Staff

Fitting into the company's culture can be important, especially in SMEs where you often have tightly-knit teams. Let candidates interact with your staff informally. Let them go for lunch together or leave them in the kitchen area with a couple of staff members for five to ten minutes to have a chat. It's quite astonishing what emerges this way.

Case Study Screening: Pret A Manger

Pret A Manger has invested in its recruitment process to make sure that the business is filled with 'Pret people' from top to bottom. Managers are told to focus on 'family trees' i.e. having the right people in the right place. The aim is to fill every vacancy within three days (for which it has an 80% success rate). The company takes the view that sales and profitability will follow if the right team is in place. This appears to be correct. In 2015 the chain reported an increase in sales of almost 14% on the previous year.

As part of the selection process, candidates work in a shop for part of a day and the team they have worked with then decide if they get the job. In 2015 Andrea Wareham, Pret's Director of People announced that in the previous six years their annual employee turnover reduced from 90% to 60% which compares well to the industry average of about 150%.

Getting the team involved and giving them ownership for part of the recruitment process makes staff have an investment in and feel responsible for the new employee. This means established colleagues spend time with the new people and help them feel comfortable, which in turn makes the new staff more likely to stay.

Predicting Success in Workplace Performance

At one stage during my employed career I worked for a delightful but decidedly eccentric manager (John) who, among other things, would regularly scupper my carefully considered, evidence-based graduate recruitment programme by injecting graduates who impressed him with their firm handshake.

A typical remark would be: "Good strong handshake - Harrrrm! Whoof! – mark of a good leader, don't you see?" (It wasn't a question and since he was a director there wasn't much I could do to argue the case. I knew it would all come out in the wash.)

The strength of a handshake is indicative of nothing so far as leadership is concerned and when these young people joined the assessment programme this became clear.

John was not alone in making this type of mistake. Most recruiting managers submit to unconscious bias and make a decision about a candidate in the first ten seconds of an interview. They spend the rest of the interview unconsciously looking for data to support their initial conclusion.

It's fairly well known that interviews which have poor data collection content and/or are conducted by untrained interviewers are a waste of time. In 'Work Rules!' Laszlo Bock suggests that as much as 99.4% of the interview time is spent trying to confirm the interviewer's initial impression.

Recruitment decisions are often based on gut feel and bias. Bias are unconscious feelings that influence our judgement of certain people. This is one area where you really **mustn't** listen to your gut instinct because it serves you badly. Research shows it does not in any way predict whether a candidate will be successful in the job.

Our bias affects us and our decision-making processes in a number of different ways:

- perception – how we see people and perceive reality;
- attitude – how we react towards certain people;
- behaviours – how receptive we are towards certain people;
- attention – which aspects of a person we pay most attention to;
- listening – how much we actively listen to what certain people say.

Unless you correct your bias, you are effectively relying on 'gut-feel'. According to Geoff Smart co-author of 'Who', most people make appointments using gut-feel. It doesn't work. Smart says it leads to about a 50% recruitment failure rate.

Google made the same mistakes as the rest of us until it realised that its attrition rate was far too high. After experimenting with different recruitment processes and measuring the success of the outcomes it settled on a process to actively remove bias. The company uses a very structured data collection process, using the same structured questions for all candidates so that the answers can be compared and using test exercises related to the work role. A number of different panel members from across the business will be involved to try and erase individual and functional bias and each candidate's responses will be collated and considered together.

The first stage is a phone/Google Hangout interview. During such interviews, candidates speak with a potential peer or manager. For software engineering roles, the discussion will last between 30 and 60 minutes. When answering coding questions, candidates talk through their thought process while writing code in a Google Doc that they share with the interviewer.

The second stage is an on-site interview. Candidates usually meet with four interviewers - some potential teammates and some cross-functional employees. The interview is about 30 to 45 minutes' duration. For software engineering candidates, the panel wants to understand the candidate's coding skills and technical areas of expertise, including tools or programming languages and general knowledge on topics like data structures and algorithms. There's generally some discussion. Candidates must be prepared to talk through their solutions in depth.

The combination of objective data collection and assessment by several interviewers has reduced Google's recruitment failure rate significantly. This is a process that SMEs can easily replicate to improve their recruitment decisions. It's neither difficult, nor expensive and it's very efficient.

Effective and Legal Data Collection

You want to know what the likelihood of a candidate performing well in the workplace is going to be. The best predictor of how someone will perform in a job is a work sample test. This entails giving candidates a sample piece of work, similar to that which they would do in the job, and assessing their performance. Even this can't predict performance perfectly, since actual performance also depends on other skills, such as how well they collaborate with others, adapt to uncertainty, and learn, but it gives very useful data.

Examples of Testing Candidates

People always ask me what I mean by 'job-related' testing so here are some examples that I have used either in our own recruitment processes or for our clients. We'll start with the data collection process we use for Trainee HR Consultants in my business.

- At stage one candidates are given some information and asked to write a short email accepting a resignation from an employee. This is a very basic task but tests the ability to write clear English accurately and whether they can correctly process a simple request. We also make one of the names slightly unusual to see if they check the spelling.

- In stage two we give applicants a short HR policy into which six mistakes have been inserted. Since most candidates won't know that much about HR there is only one technical error. The rest are grammar and spelling errors. There's no time limit. Most people aren't naturally detail-conscious but there are coping strategies for overcoming a lack of detail-consciousness, so we give candidates time to check and re-check. Despite this the average applicant spots only one error out of a possible six.

- At stage three we ask candidates to carry out pre-interview preparation. This is to research a current employment topic and be prepared to make a short presentation to us about it. It tests the ability to research, understand and analyse the data and be able to explain it both during the presentation and during the questioning afterwards. The process tests conscientiousness and potentially intellectual curiosity as well. A candidate who puts the effort in here is really valuable, especially if he finds it an interesting challenge. It's always worth asking how the candidate felt about the process. If he replies that it was quite hard but he nevertheless found it interesting or rewarding that's a plus.

Here are some other examples of selection testing.

- Bus drivers. The first check is whether they can physically fit into the cab (some people have very short legs or long bodies and they can't reach the pedals.) If they exceed the load-bearing limit of the driver's seat the application is not progressed. If they physically fit they are asked to drive a vehicle round the block accompanied by an instructor.

- Data controller. Asked to prepare and present a ten-minute training session on the data control software.
- Marketing co-ordinator. Asked to research a product, prepare an outline marketing plan for the product to be used in the company's online shop and present it.
- Customer service. Staff who work principally on the phone are asked to take part in a phone role play.
- Warehouse staff. Asked to pick and pack certain items to see how they handle them and whether they can physically manage weights or difficult shapes.
- In some cases applicants are asked to make and submit a video of them doing something. For example, in the case of prospective trainers for the charity Dogs for Good candidates are asked to show how they train their own dog.

I have referred to other examples of testing in the various case studies throughout this book.

The second-best predictors of performance are aptitude tests, which examine general cognitive ability. In contrast to brainteasers, these are actual tests with defined right and wrong answers, similar to what you might find in an IQ test. They are predictive because general cognitive ability includes the capacity to learn, and the combination of raw intelligence and learning ability will make most people successful in most jobs.

The use of structured interviews, where candidates are asked a consistent set of questions with clear criteria to assess the quality of responses, will also elicit useful evidence-based information. Structured interviews revolve around competence-based questions asking candidates to describe prior achievements and match those to what is required in the current job, for example, "Tell me about a time when ..?" Competence-based structured interviews are predictive even for jobs that are themselves unstructured.

The best way to obtain data for recruitment purposes is to use a combination of assessment techniques. For example, a test of general cognitive ability when combined with an assessment of conscientiousness is better able to predict who will be successful in a job. People who score high on conscientiousness won't stop until a job is done rather than stopping at 'good enough'. They are more likely to feel responsibility for their teams and the environment around them.

Aptitude Tests

Aptitude tests can be very powerful predictors of future work performance. Typically aptitude tests include questions in verbal, numerical and abstract reasoning.

Candidates who have a high level of cognitive ability can:

- perform work tasks more accurately and efficiently;
- make decisions more effectively;
- use reasoning skills and solve problems;
- respond intelligently to new or complex circumstances.

The resulting score reflects candidates' ability to acquire, retain, organise and apply information in a variety of circumstances. By comparing your candidates' scores to a relevant normative group, you can accurately predict their potential job performance.

You can compare their results with comparator groups. For example:

- employed adults;

- an industry group (such as call centre, legal profession, retail or trade);
- people who work at a particular level (such as graduates, entry-level managers or senior-level managers);
- a group of your own top performers.

N.B.: While aptitude tests are very helpful, there are many free aptitude tests online so some candidates will practice in advance. Use aptitude tests as a way of gaining additional data and calibrate it with other forms of testing and structured interviews to assess the aptitude data independently.

Personality Profiling

One way of assessing personality style is to use a personality profile. It's important to understand that there are no 'right' and 'wrong' personalities, but there may be clusters of personality scales that you might expect to see or not to see in particular jobs. For example, you would expect a senior finance person to score highly in detail consciousness, data awareness and meeting deadlines. On the other hand a senior operations person would probably score lower in detail consciousness (too much of this might indicate a micro-manager) but may score highly on planning and problem solving. Each case will turn on its own facts. If you do get something unexpected, explore it within the interview. There may be a very reasonable explanation.

The following are some of the most frequently used personality profile tools.

- Thomas International – DISC. The DISC Personality Profile is based on the work of psychologist Dr Williams Moulton Marston, and was introduced in his 1928 book *Emotions of*

Normal People. Dr Marston developed the DISC Personality Profile after studying the personality. DISC looks at behaviour, temperament, and personality. A DISC profile provides a comprehensive overview of the way that people think, act, and interact. The DISC assessment was developed as a tool to measure four primary behavioural traits: dominance, influence, steadiness and conscientiousness.

- The Myers-Briggs Type Indicator (MBTI) assessment is designed to measure preferences in how people see the world and make decisions. It was developed in the 1940s by Katharine Cook Briggs and her daughter, Isabel Briggs Myers, who thought that an understanding of personality preferences would help women who were entering the workforce for the first time to identify the sort of war-time jobs which would suit them best. By the early 1960s, the initial questionnaire had become refined into the MBTI. The MBTI uses a series of forced choice questions in which the individual has to choose only one of two possible answers to each question. The choices are a mixture of word pairs and short statements and are chosen to reflect opposite preferences. Participants may skip questions if they feel they are unable to choose.

- The SHL OPQ32r test measures aspects of behaviour that are crucial to performance potential, which cannot easily be identified by other techniques, such as reading CVs and interviewing. The OPQ32r provides a clear, simple framework for understanding the impact of personality on job performance. It is available in more than 30 languages and is administered online. The questionnaire takes the majority of people less than 30 minutes to complete and a range of reports are available, providing clear, concise, graphical summaries of performance against job competencies. Most of these reports are designed for use by line managers.

Structured Interviews

The goal of your interview process should be to predict how candidates will perform once they join the team. Interviewers often use questions such as: "Tell me about yourself." "What is your greatest weakness?" "What is your greatest strength?" The answers to questions like these don't tell you if the candidates can do the job.

Some companies use rather surreal problems, such as: "Your client is a paper manufacturer that is considering building a second plant. Should they?" These don't work either.

Use your job description and person specification or Smart and Street's scorecard to write some structured questions which are relevant to the role. Ask candidates to take an example of an actual relevant experience and ask a number of follow up probing questions. N.B.: Avoid situational interviews which present a job-related hypothetical situation, for example, "What would you do if … ?"

Questions to Use in a Structured Interview

Asking competency-based questions in a structured interview gives you the chance to probe in some detail into a candidate's actual experience. Because the candidate will be drawing on memory you are more likely to get to the truth.

You have to prepare questions which are appropriate for the level and type of role. Prepare an initial question which relates to the role for which you are recruiting. The question asks the candidate to draw on his actual experience to provide evidence as to experience in an area relevant to the job or of a skill set relevant to the job.

Here are some examples of structured interview questions.

- Tell me about a specific time when you had to assist your staff in understanding the relevance to the organisation of an aspect of their work. (Follow ups: What mechanisms did you use to communicate with them? How effective was the communication? How did you evaluate that effectiveness?)
- Tell me about a time when you effectively managed your team to achieve a goal. What did your approach look like? (Follow-ups: What were your targets and how did you meet them as an individual and as a team? How did you adapt your leadership approach to different individuals? What was the key takeaway from this specific situation?)
- Tell me about a time you had difficulty working with someone (can be a colleague, classmate or client). What made this person difficult to work with for you? (Follow-ups: What steps did you take to resolve the problem? What was the outcome? What could you have done differently?)
- What single project or task would you consider the most significant accomplishment in your career so far?
- In relation to this project tell me about the company, your title, your position, your role, and the team.
- What were the actual results achieved?
- When did it take place and how long did the project take?
- Why you were chosen to play the role you did?
- What were the three or four biggest challenges you faced and how did you deal with them?
- Where did you go the extra mile or take the initiative?
- Walk me through the plan, how you managed to it, and if it was successful.
- Describe the environment and resources.
- Describe your manager's style and whether you liked it or not.

- Describe the technical skills needed to accomplish the objective and how they were used.
- What were some of the biggest mistakes you made?
- What aspects of the [named] project did you really enjoy?
- What aspects of the [named] project did you not really like? How did you handle them?
- How were you managed and influenced others when you worked on the [named] project, with examples.
- How were you managed, coached, and influenced by others when you worked on the [named] project, with lots of examples.
- What you would do differently if you could do it again?
- What type of formal recognition did you receive?
- What was it about your work that made you most satisfied at your last place of employment?

The following questions are particular favourites at Russell HR Consulting.

- How do you keep up-to-date with your industry?

If the candidate is unable to cite any personal or professional development he's done of late, it is definitely a red flag as far as passion and conscientiousness are concerned. Those who really care about what they do, spend extra time outside working hours to better their skills and develop their knowledge. The genuinely enthusiastic would probably smile and have a spark in their eye when answering this question.

This interview question will help you assess a fit for workplace culture.

- Give three of your key work-related values. Share examples of situations where you demonstrated these values.

Here are some ways of assessing intellectual curiosity.

- Tell me about something you have taught yourself in the last six months. Why did you do it? How did you go about teaching yourself this new skill or idea, and what was the result?
- Before the interview, give candidates a task that requires some research, and see how in-depth their study is. This is also a good way of assessing conscientiousness. Ask candidates to talk you through how they approached the task, how long it took to do the research and prepare the presentation and how they tested it.
- Ask what questions they have for you. Curious people will ask thoughtful questions.

Growth Mindset

Our workplace is extremely interesting and stimulating, but it has its challenges. For fixed mindset people it could well be stressful because we're juggling so much and there's a lot at stake. For people who are tough-minded and see making mistakes simply as way to learn, it's a fabulous place to thrive and grow. We therefore look for people with a growth mindset outlook. Here are some examples of the sorts of questions we ask.

- Tell me about a time when you got bogged down at work and found it hard to move on and achieve your goals.
- What was the situation?
- What caused the problem?
- How did you feel about it?
- What happened and what was the outcome?
- Looking back what would you do differently? What did you learn from it?

You will find some useful structured questions you can adapt for your own purposes at:

www.va/gov/pbi/questions.asp

Use Technology to Help You

The right applicant tracking system (ATS) will make your recruitment process more efficient. Not all ATSs are the same and different systems suit different businesses.

The benefits of an ATS are as follows.

- They organise the application process into stages. These can range from 'CV received' to 'Arrange first Interview' and 'Unsuccessful' and this means that you can move applicants between the stages. This is an easy and clear way to review applicants and keep a record of them, so if you have a vacancy in the future you could refer back to the 'Shortlist' or the 'Keep in mind' sections for future hires.
- Once in the relevant stage, communication templates stored on the system can be sent out, making it easier to advise applicants of the outcome of their application. This means that engagement with the applicant is easy to manage and monitor.
- Most ATSs will have an online interview booking facility. Some give both company users and applicants the access to an online interview booking facility which is integrated with Microsoft Office. This means that everyone can organise and coordinate the process to best suit each party without the need for phone calls.
- You are able to create a report specifically for your business. A report could take the shape of monitoring the success of job boards so you know where the majority of your applicants are coming from etc.

I have included some suggestions in the 'Further Reading and Resources' section.

Unsuccessful Candidates

Recruitment is your shop window and it's important that you treat candidates courteously. For those candidates that are unsuccessful, let them know the outcome and be prepared to give some feedback. They may not be suitable now, but they might be in a year or two. The effect of social media means that if you slip-up your mistake can be horribly public.

You may remember how in February 2014 the curator of the Sherlock Holmes Museum, Andrea von Ehrenstein, responded somewhat bizarrely when a prospective candidate, Rachel Fox, asked some additional questions about a vacancy there. Ms von Ehrenstein's email seemed to suggest Ms Fox was thoughtless and lazy. The story was repeated on Twitter and by the end of the day everyone had heard about this very odd exchange. This type of thing can damage a company's reputation and branding.

Takeaways: Chapter 6
Assess Applications Effectively

- Devise an efficient data collection process.
- Use structured interviews which question and allow you to probe into the candidate's competence.
- Use work-related testing to capture and assess relevant data.
- Use technology to streamline your process.

Treat all candidates courteously, whether they have been successful or unsuccessful.

YOUR NOTES

_____

_____

_____

_____

_____

_____

_____

_____

_____

_____

_____

_____

_____

_____

Chapter 7
Different Talent Pools

Managing Talent across the Generations

You will have read or heard about 'baby boomers', 'generation X' and 'generation Y' (also known as 'millennials'). It's said that generalisations are odious and generational characterisations are as flawed as any other stereotype as they don't account for differences between individuals. But although the definitions are artificial, generation groupings can be useful concepts. For one thing, they allow us to understand how the manager-employee dynamic is evolving, and how management techniques could – or should – be adjusted accordingly.

Employers are currently managing four generations of employees and they've all been given nicknames by which they are commonly known:

- silents (born between 1925 and 1946);
- baby boomers (born between 1946 and 1964);
- generation Xers (born between 1965 and 1980);
- generation Ys or millennials (born 1980 onwards).

Each group has its own distinct characteristics, values and attitudes towards work, based on their life experiences. To integrate these different generations into the workplace successfully, you must make changes in recruitment and benefits, creating a corporate culture to demonstrate respect for and inclusion of each element of your multi-generational work force.

Silents

Silents are considered to be the most loyal workers. They are highly dedicated and the most risk averse. Their values were shaped by the Great Depression, World War II, and the post-war boom years. Silents have a strong commitment to teamwork and collaboration. This group has the most affluent elderly population in history because of their willingness to conserve and save after recovering from the financial impact of the post-war period.

Baby Boomers

The baby boomers ('boomers') are hardworking and motivated by position, perks and prestige. They want to succeed and have the trappings to go with it. They are prepared to work long hours and define themselves by their professional accomplishments. Since they sacrificed a great deal to get where they are in their career, they may criticise younger workers for a poor work ethic and low level of workplace commitment.

Boomers tend to be confident, independent and self-reliant. They grew up in an era of reform, questioning established authority systems and challenging the status quo. They had better educational and financial opportunities than the silent group and are achievement-oriented, dedicated and career-focused. They welcome exciting, challenging projects and strive to make a difference. Since they equate work and position with self-worth, they are quite competitive in the workplace. They are intuitive, resourceful and strive to win.

Boomers believe in hierarchal structure and may have a hard time adjusting to workplace flexibility trends. They believe in 'face-time' at the office and may fault younger generations for working remotely.

Generation X

As women flooded into the workplace, the birth rate dropped substantially, resulting in the baby-bust. The Generation X group ('Xers') is 25% smaller than the boomers. Many Xers grew up as 'latch key' kids, home alone after school while both of their parents worked, and/ or they were raised by a single parent.

Xers saw their parents devoting long hours to the workplace, often sacrificing time at home with their families. In the economic downturn of the 1980s, many of these hard workers lost their jobs. In consequence Xers learned to become more pragmatic about work, wanted more life-work balance and were often cynical about a lack of employer loyalty.

As employees Xers want to have clear statements of goals, but be allowed reasonable latitude on how to achieve those goals. Build on their interest in gaining new skills and knowledge by providing opportunities to grow on the job. They tend to have a 'work hard, play hard' mentality. Give them the opportunities to make choices. Since this generation has become accustomed to fending for themselves, provide options, for example, for task selection, options for challenges, to formulate new processes, and to develop creative yet appropriate conclusions. Allow them the freedom to use their own resourcefulness and creativity to achieve success. Strong, relationship-oriented mentorships are of great value to Xers.

Provide competitive pay. Although money isn't the biggest motivator for Xers, it's definitely a factor, especially considering their stage in life, with responsibilities such as property ownership, parenthood and children entering college. Results-based bonuses can be a great way to reward them without committing to a permanent salary increase.

Provide a strong vision and a good reputation to attract Xers. Promote your business's mission and vision as part of your marketing. Since Xers want to make a difference, a company that makes a difference in its industry, community or the world generally will have an edge in appealing to them.

Generation "Why"?

Generation Y workers ('millennials') are completely different from all other employees. They've been referred to as 'lazy' and 'the most high-maintenance workforce in the history of work'. They are certainly different, but it's perhaps unfair to describe them quite so harshly. They have their own ideas about workplaces and aren't shy about expressing them. All that in-your-face "aren't I great?" and know-it-all attitude can be trying for the more traditional worker.

Millennials have often been called the 'trophy kids' because on sports teams and in school, each child, regardless of capability, when provided a chance to contribute and perform, was often given some kind of a certificate or award just for having participated. Previous generations received credit only when they won.

These children were praised lavishly by their parents and teachers, who had high levels of hope and expectations for positive outcomes. Millennials were involved in many activities concurrently: lessons, sports, social events, playgroups and teams. They are sometimes described as the 'over-scheduled' generation.

Since millennials form a significant part of the workforce and that part is only going to get bigger, you can't ignore them. The smart approach is to harness their positives (there are plenty!), find out how to manage their less attractive traits and learn to go with the flow.

They are a very mobile group of workers. In the 2016 Deloitte survey, which researches millennials' values, ambitions and drivers of job satisfaction, the results indicated that one in four millennials would leave their current employment to join a new organisation or to do something else during the next year if the opportunity arose. Given that you're probably going to invest heavily in terms of training and development, that mobility could present a risk.

So how do we manage this group of butterflies? They have completely different work values when compared to previous groups of workers. Step one is to understand their drivers.

Meaningful work, good salary and financial benefits are the most important employment motivator, followed by work-life balance and opportunities to develop their careers and take on leadership roles. About 33% of millennials will place flexibility over salary when considering a job offer.

The traditional motivators are less important. For them learning and developing their skills is key. They are ambitious, and they want to have a say in how things are done and led.

- They love change and variety within a structured environment.
- They think they can do anything and want to have the chance to prove it.
- They want to work in socially-responsible workplaces.
- They are the most technologically advanced group of employees and are skilled multitaskers.

- They want immediate access to information and need plenty of stimuli.

Knowing this, there are a number of things you can do to get the best out of millennials and keep them engaged. Millennials want leaders who place the most emphasis on employee development, well-being and growth rather than simply controlling the work experience.

Coach, train and mentor them. Let them ask questions. Provide advice and information and give regular feedback to them. Millennials want to know how they're doing and what they can do to improve. Frequent feedback helps them develop and increases their sense of being valued. Feed their curiosity and set them projects that will develop their skills.

Involve them and listen to them. Millennials may well ask "why?" before doing a task. This might drive the older worker mad, but it's a reasonable question. They're not saying they won't do it, just asking for the rationale and that's fair enough. They love to be part of the decision-making process too. Bear in mind that they have been consulted by their parents and teachers since they were knee-high to a grasshopper so simply directing them and expecting them to follow unquestioningly won't work well. They often have good ideas, so let them be part of creative and problem-solving processes.

They love a challenge. They've been brought up to think they can do anything, so stretch them. Give them variety and interest. Having people who aren't afraid of tough assignments is fantastic. They might get it wrong, but that's all part of learning. Help them understand what to do next to get it right, dust them down and get them back on the horse.

Millennials love structure so build a framework into your workplace. Within that framework, give them some freedom. Provide guidance and feedback, but don't micro-manage them.

Not everybody likes working in a team but millennials do. They believe that working as a team can accomplish more. Team exercises and activities motivate these employees. This can be anything from an activity such as a team lunch, a social activity or team sporting or fitness target to a team training session.

Millennials have grown up with the internet, smartphones, broadband, mobile devices and social media being the norm. They expect instant access to information. Boomers and Xers just haven't had the exposure the millennials have. Use their love and knowledge of technology to your advantage. Allow them to suggest ways to make your business a more technically savvy place.

Strategies for Cross-Generational Leadership

As these four generations continue to interact, companies can no longer assume that traditional benefits (high pay, pension, car, medical insurance etc.) will secure the best people. You also have to consider their individual preferences and adapt your management style. As more silents retire, boomers seek post-retirement careers, Xers demand challenging but balanced work assignments, and millennials expect high perks in exchange for loyalty and technological savvy, you must find creative ways to recruit and retain talent.

The different groups have different outlooks, different priorities and different motivators, and these will clash from time to time. Traits that Xers have traditionally seen as strengths create discord with millennials. Xers tend to be hierarchical, seeking authority to make decisions and preferring formal processes. This is a strength in that they can guide people through workplace procedures, but it's also a weakness if team members don't want to operate in a hierarchy. And millennials, by and large, don't.

Similarly, Xers value individual contributions and encourage employees to work under their own steam. Millennials need more instruction. Xers' reluctance to spoon-feed younger colleagues is one of the greatest difficulties in their management style. They take the view "Nobody held my hand! Why should I hold your hand?" This becomes an issue because younger employees, who feel a great sense of uncertainty about their professional roles and career prospects and need much greater day-to-day engagement from their immediate managers.

The answer comes down to communication and how managers inform, instruct and advise their teams. Experts agree that one of the most effective ways for Xers to improve their management of other peer groups is to become more flexible communicators, being mindful of the unique needs of both boomers and millennials. The former expect a more formal approach and a willingness to communicate face-to-face; the latter also want more face-time, but whereas boomers want their managers to simply tell them what to do, millennials favour a collaborative approach in which goals and processes are developed together.

When it comes to written communication Xers are better equipped to communicate with boomers than with millennials. Boomers drill deep; millennials take in a lot of information over a broad range and skim. Xers take in less information, but still drill deep. This means managing upwards is fine, but when Xers need to manage millennials, they are managing their opposites.

Boomers tend to rely on data, a thinking style of management and decision-making. Millennials prefer a more intuitive and instinctive form of communication. The challenge for Xers is to communicate simultaneously in a thinking style (data-evidence argument) and intuitively (real experiences, bullet point style).

Most companies rely too heavily on one strategy for corporate communication. By making the same message available in multiple formats (thereby increasing the number of times you communicate a message), you'll ensure that you reach all workers. Silents and boomers may appreciate verbal communication about changes in policy or procedures, while Xers and millennials may prefer the use of e-mail, instant messages, or corporate broadcasts.

A good way to get people to work together across the generations is to provide them with an opportunity to educate each other about each generation's own history, characteristics, milestone events, culture, language and norms.

Make sure all groups are constantly mentored. As more established and experienced workers move towards retirement, develop processes to ensure there is a transfer of knowledge and capture of organisational memory. The more structure you build into your mentoring programme to create knowledge transfer the better. First determine younger employees' goals and developmental needs, and then pair them with older, more experienced employees to create cross-organisational conversation between them.

Consider various mentoring models: one-on-one sessions, group programmes, senior leadership discussion panels, and a 'speed mentoring' programme where employees sit across from company experts to ask questions. No matter what method you choose, making mentoring a part of the employment life cycle will ensure that the company's history and knowledge continues from one generation to the next.

Encourage managers to develop strong interpersonal skills to foster relationships with employees and each other. One of your key responsibilities is to ensure that everyone in the business understands that working together effectively is not an option but a requirement. Create a courteous, thoughtful, open and inclusive environment where workers of all ages and cultural backgrounds can share who they are without fear of being judged, 'fixed,' or changed.

Be open to new ideas and provide regular feedback, working with managers and staff to shape the company's strategic vision. Be open to different perspectives based on generational attitudes.

Consider compensation and benefits to satisfy the needs of each generation's viewpoint, attitudes, and values about work. For example, as people retire later in life, many will want more time off as opposed to increased compensation. Xers like companies that offer high financial rewards. Younger people may value more flexibility, such as assignments that foster new skill sets they can apply later in their careers.

With the variety of multigenerational employees in today's workplace, companies can no longer stick to traditional rules of leadership and management. Businesses can achieve real strategic advantage by embracing the diversity among generations to create a flexible work environment that values all people and keeps them productive, regardless of age.

Case Study Managing Millennials: England Hockey

In common with many modern organisations England Hockey ('EH') has a flat management structure so the ability to move up can stall much earlier in an employee's career because the opportunities for promotion are greatly reduced. As an organisation in which one-third of its employees is a millennial, the majority of whom are at officer level, retention is a challenge. Research suggests that millennials are focused on self-direction, work-life balance, fulfilment, as well as benefits and perks and especially learning and development. They thrive on opportunities to be creative and look for leadership, responsibility and the chance to lead projects.

With this in mind, and with a focus on personal development, expanding influence and broadening and deepening skills, EH established its Stepping Up To Management Programme ('SUMP') for officers as a means of maintaining engagement levels and improving retention.

Officers are not managers but generally have some responsibility for particular work streams or projects. For instance, an officer in adult participation will run certain campaigns to promote hockey, which in turn will encourage adults to play more. SUMP gives officers the opportunity to develop their skills, lead projects and be prepared to take that next step when it does materialise. For example, officers can step up to manage a team of volunteers or an area outside their usual work sphere. Leading discrete projects means they can manage the work flow, timetable and budgets, collaborating and developing and implementing EH's Employer Value Proposition.

The managers of SUMP participants are also doing some training so they know how they can engage better with their teams in recognising skills and identifying projects in which an officer can take the lead. EH has a huge events portfolio which is the ideal opportunity for giving temporary management responsibility for the duration of an event.

Entry to the SUMP programme is not automatic. Prospective participants must be identified by their manager and the case made as to why they should be included. Applications are endorsed by the department Director and then reviewed by CEO, Sally Munday, and HR Manager, Michele Townsend. A decision is made based on their management potential as well as looking at the applicants' commitment to the behaviours and values of the organisation, the quality of the work and length of service.

The SUMP programme includes modules around personal style and skills, helping the participants get to grips with the management skills they need to develop in the business. SUMP is very visibly supported by senior management, including time spent with Sally during the programme. There is input from internal functions such as finance, commercial, ethics and compliance and HR, as well as line managers and technical input from external training providers. Between the modules there are mentoring and reflective practice meetings, together with discussions and processes to put learning into practice. As the programme moves on, participants start working on projects outside their normal work stream.

Michele said: "One of the things that is important to a millennial is the sense of purpose of the organisation they work for. We're fortunate that EH is a National Governing Body employing individuals with a passion for sport! As part of this programme, the participants will develop EH's Employer Value Proposition for our website, which will be used as the basis for all our recruitment going forward. This project will encompass what it's like to work for our organisation, what we can offer and why EH is a great place to work!"

Takeaways: Chapter 7 Different Talent Pools

- Be aware of the different requirements for managing different generations of employees and manage accordingly.
- Communicate effectively and make your message available in multiple formats.
- Encourage mentoring and allow them to educate each other.
- Monitor all groups.
- Consider compensation and benefits to satisfy the needs of each group.

YOUR NOTES

Chapter 8
Recruitment Case Studies

Does all the stuff I've been talking about work? The short answer is 'yes'. Here are some examples.

The HR Consultant

When I said that the dearth of really good people is damaging UK business I included my own business, Russell HR Consulting, in my remark. We have developed good assessment and training processes. We are still working on sourcing the talent and I am pursuing some of the ideas I researched and found for this book!

A number of years ago we had a complete revolution in the way we recruit our people. I found that traditionally qualified HR people did not transition well into our environment, so we started to look for people who were the right raw material, ideally with general business experience, and trained them.

We had been developing a very structured training process consisting of a number of modules. Each module asked the trainee to research and be able to answer about 50 questions. If the trainee could answer all the questions he would have a really broad base of knowledge. We have an excellent technical library to support self-learning and trainees were encouraged to read relevant newsletters.

We do Tool Box Talks once a week when I leap to my feet and do a half-an-hour session in front of the white board in the office. The team love this because it's extremely informal and usually very topical, picking up and looking at something we've dealt with that week. It gives us a great opportunity to explore matters in a very relaxed environment together. Remember, millennials love team activities.

Every month we have a Lunchtime Learning session where we have lunch together, often with an invited guest. Our trainees (suitably fortified by a strong cuppa) do a ten-minute presentation on the subject they've been working on and are grilled (nicely!) by the team and guest. You'd be surprised how popular this is.

Added to these learning activities, our trainees have the opportunity to work-shadow senior consultants, spend time at client sites, do some off-site training and give advice under supervised conditions.

Kirsty at SAE 2016

Kirsty really enjoyed spending some time with one of our logistics clients. Having spent time in the warehouse, going out with a driver and in the office, she feels that she understands far more about the business now.

We often have informal discussions about work questions and our workspace is set up to allow these conversations to break out easily and spontaneously. Trainees are encouraged to keep asking questions.

I have an operational background and worked as a retail catering manager for several years before specialising. This experience gives me a considerable advantage when dealing with other business owners because I have had the same problems and can put myself in their shoes. For this reason we create opportunities for our team members to go out to spend time with clients. It means they get to know the client, they find out about the specific business and they learn about the sector more generally. It's interesting, good for their development, making them better consultants, but it also helps build trust with our clients that we really understand their business.

We constantly refresh and add to our training process. We work so closely together during this process that in consequence our consultants absorb not just knowledge but the values of the business.

With all this in place, we recruit people who demonstrate intelligence, intellectual curiosity, conscientiousness, detail consciousness, a certain mental and emotional toughness and humility. If they have these qualities the rest can be trained.

I seriously hate interviewing. You can waste such a lot of time seeing the wrong people, so my priority was to develop a process which collected data from the moment candidates started the process. I didn't want anyone who was not really good quality to set foot in the door. All candidates receive a detailed information pack and in the pack we clearly say that applications must be accompanied by a covering letter that sets out evidence showing they have the essential requirements. We go so far as to say that if they don't do this they won't be considered for interview. About 90% of applicants ignore this. Since detail consciousness and compliance are both critical qualities all 90% are regretted.

The 10% who get this right are usually fairly good. We invite them to a phone screening and do some remote testing. If they get through that they are invited to the last stage where they have to research and make a short presentation, do a personality questionnaire, further testing for detail consciousness and a structured interview. We usually end the process by taking candidates for lunch (it's surprising what data emerges when the candidate is relaxed). All team members get involved at some stage and are able to contribute their views. It also helps to calibrate data and remove unconscious bias.

We are always willing to provide feedback to unsuccessful candidates. The feedback we have had from candidates is generally approving of our process. They find it robust and relevant but not too long.

The TrustMark CEO

TrustMark is the Government-endorsed quality scheme operating under licence from the Department for Business, Innovation and Skills that signposts people to reputable local tradespeople. It provides consumers with impartial assessments through a continually expanding database and telephone helpline.

In 2014 we were asked to create a recruitment process for a new CEO and to manage it in conjunction with the Board. When the job was advertised candidates received an information pack by email. The first part of the selection process asked candidates to submit an application form, a covering letter and a paper of 1,500 words discussing the following: "*What are your views on the pros and cons of a centralised government licensing scheme for tradespeople?*"

Based on evidence demonstrated in the applications and discussion paper, a number of candidates were shortlisted and asked to attend structured interviews and do some testing. These interviews were carefully structured and conducted by board members in panels of two.

The Russell HR team wrote the questions to assess and test specified areas, based on the requirements of the job description and the person specification. Each interviewer took a specific area of questioning and both members of the panel took notes and scored the answers. Candidates were scored as follows:

0. No evidence or negative evidence
1. Some evidence
2. Adequate evidence
3. Evidence exceeds requirement

From the results of the testing and structured interviews, four candidates were shortlisted and invited to an assessment day.

The Board wanted to include some elements of testing which reflected activities the CEO would carry out. The assessment day started with a group debate. Each candidate had a brief and had to influence and persuade the other members of the group, overcoming objections to try and carry his view.

After the debate, the candidates were asked to analyse and present some financial information and there was a further structured interview.

By the time the data had been gathered the Board had a significant amount of data and was able to make a well-informed choice which has proved to be a good indicator of performance.

Published by kind permission of TrustMark.

The Sales Representative

Sales people are tricky to recruit. Predicting successful performance in the workplace is difficult because salespeople are often very good at selling themselves. This is not necessarily an accurate predictor of an ability to sell the company's products. In fact, over the course of a year I dismiss a considerable number of sales people who can't or won't sell.

BioHorizons' General Manager, Ken O'Brien, has developed a process which is challenging for candidates but a good predictor of success.

At the first stage Ken sits informally with candidates on a one-to-one basis for half-an-hour or so, having a coffee and a chat. He does some exploration around the skill sets for the job, but the main purpose is to get to know candidates at a more personal level and find out how likeable they are. This is a role where the job holder will need to build up relationships so the ability to influence, persuade and get on with others is critical. It also gives candidates the chance to find out a bit more about the company and decide if they want to continue with the selection process.

The second stage is a more structured interview process. About two weeks before the interview Ken gives candidates a scenario related to the role. He asks them to research one of the products to enable them to participate in a sales role play. Product information is quite complex so it takes effort and time to get to grips with it to a level sufficient to enable a candidate to discuss it reasonably fluently.

Preparing for this is hard work and there is usually a 50% drop-out rate at this stage. For those who do the work the ability to predict future success of the candidates is much clearer. The following information becomes apparent.

- The ability to learn.
- The willingness to learn.
- The ability to correctly grasp the key facts about the product.
- The ability to apply and discuss accurately what has been learned.
- The level of conscientiousness.

Around 30% of the remaining 50% succeed at this stage.

This process has improved the quality of the sales team and increased retention rates. Since BioHorizons introduced this two-step process only one sales person who went through it has left, compared with seven who were selected using the more traditional unstructured interview in the same period.

There are two benefits for new employees too. The first is that they have already got to grips with one of the products they will be selling. That enables them to hit the ground running in at least one area and reduces the amount of time overall before they are fully effective.

The second is slightly unexpected. Ken has found that because they have already proved their mettle to some extent through the process they have the recruitment experience in common with other members of the sales team. It helps them to bond and start to build internal relationships.

Ken added the following coda: "Those who have come through the process have proven to be self-starters on territory and been very consistent in their return, whilst the ones who did not come through that process need more coaching. This isn't saying that one is better than another but the self-starters have a drive to succeed no matter what management guidance they get."

Published by kind permission of BioHorizons.

The Barber

Michael Debnam is the owner of a successful barber shop in Hitchin, called Men at Work. Michael has found that even qualified barbers are sometimes lacking in skill. (Michael's phrase: "They might have a certificate but they can't even hold a pair of scissors!").

Interviews didn't tell Michael whether the candidate will be a good barber. Now when he has a selection interview Michael asks the candidate to come in with a friend ready to cut the friend's hair. This demonstrates the level of skill, speed and overall capability of the candidate. It's a good predictor of skill. Some are great, but in some cases the cutting has been so bad Michael has to take over and correct the cut in order to prevent a "bad hair day" rift between friends.

Published by kind permission of Men at Work.

Takeaways: Chapter 8 Recruitment Case Studies

- The HR Consultant.
- The TrustMark CEO.
- The Sales Representative.
- The Barber.

YOUR NOTES

Chapter 9 On-boarding

'On-boarding' is the current phrase for bringing people into the business. It always makes me think of surfing and in some ways that's a good analogy. Get them trained and up on the surfboard they'll sail elegantly into your business. If you don't prepare them properly and take them through some well-planned processes you'll have some soggy and disgruntled recruits on your hands who may well leave.

After recruitment on-boarding has the highest business impact of all of HR practices. The way you bring people into the business is just as important as recruiting the right talent. High quality on-boarding confirms the business' employer brand image and has a high return on investment. For example, Google found that an employee who goes through a good quality on-boarding process will be effective 25% faster.

- 90% of new recruits decide whether to stay at the company within the first six months of starting a new job (Bersin Deloitte).
- 33% actively start to look for a new job within the first six months. The proportion is even higher among millennials.
- 32% of new employees are less likely to leave if they participate in an employee-centred on-boarding process rather than a company-focused one (Wall Street Journal).

- 66% of new hires are likely to stay longer than three years with a well-structured on-boarding programme (US Department of Labor).

The processes that have proved to have most impact on bringing an employee into the business successfully and making him fully productive quickly are as follows.

1. Have a role and responsibilities discussion with the new employee.
2. Match the new employee with a peer buddy.
3. Help the new employee build a social network.
4. Set up on-boarding check-ins once a month for the new employee's first six months.
5. Encourage open dialogue.

Engage With New Recruits Early (Pre-boarding)

Typically, on-boarding has been about providing the physical things a new employee needs to start working: security badge, laptop, desk assignment, setup of an email account and payroll arrangements to name a just a few. None of this generally happens until the person walks through the door on the first day.

As soon as you've found the right person and he has accepted a job offer, start the on-boarding process. You can and should reinforce your employer brand before the new employee's start date. This is just the start of an engagement process to ensure the reality of the organisation matches the brand the employee bought into.

For example, provide early online access to the paperwork which will have to be filled out a day or two after the candidate has accepted a role with you. You can also give online access to general company policies as well as benefits packages that new employees can review at their leisure. This will help them to become more familiar with your company and to feel less overwhelmed if there is a large amount of paperwork on the first day of work.

Here are some examples of pre-boarding activities.

- Before an employee's official first day, Ernst & Young provides an on-boarding portal that includes an online virtual tour that gives new employees information about the company. It takes them through the on-boarding process and answers the questions that have been most frequently asked by previous new employees.
- At MasterCard, immediately after new employees are appointed, they receive a welcome email which includes links to company videos, and access to a website where they can update their employment information, upload a photo for their badge, read about learning opportunities and complete paperwork in relation to pay and benefits. The new employee's manager can also go online to select the tools and office space he will need, so everything will be ready for him on his first day.
- US optometrist Warby Parker sends an electronic welcome packet, with the company history, core values, press clippings and what a new employee should expect during his first day, week and month. The night before they start, new employees receive a phone call from their direct supervisor to make sure that they know where to go when they arrive and confirming the time.

Day One

Typical introductions to a new business shower new employees with information, often in quite a boring way.

Working memory, a more active version of short-term memory, refers to the temporary storage of information and relates to the information we can pay attention to and manipulate. Research shows that most people can't remember more than a few things at any one time, perhaps as low as a four. (Source: Cowan N, Rouder J, Morey R, *Proceedings of the National Academy of Sciences*. 2014).

With this in mind, you have to stagger the information you want new employees to take in over a period of time to get the best results. The focus of the first day should be on introducing new employees to the key people who can help them succeed at their job, not on procedures or training manuals.

Start by introducing them to their immediate team, their manager, and colleagues with whom they will work closely. They can get to know other members of staff through break times and training. Take steps to support this process by:

- involving the new employee in group activities with peers;
- arranging team lunches with colleagues;
- organising team-building activities involving other team members;
- people tend to forget the names and roles of their new colleagues even after they have been introduced, so provide some form of crib sheet that your new employee can refer to.

Dump the Deadly Dull Stuff

Traditional on-boarding with its extensive reading and apparently endless forms can be dull and it makes people switch off. Use a variety of formats and styles to make the way you get the information across more engaging. For topics like presenting the company's story, mission and values a good, short video can go a long way as an alternative to text or PowerPoint presentation. You can make videos using tools like Pow Toon (powtoon.com) and GoAnimate (goanimate.com) at very low cost. With a bit of thought these can be funny, cool and informative.

Farmfoods Ltd created an on-boarding programme consisting of high quality, custom-made e-learning modules incorporating relevant work scenarios and helpful guidance, supported by on-the-job training and printed workbooks, as part of a blended induction approach. Employees can access the training on a smartphone or tablet, which was particularly attractive for the incoming millennial workforce.

Make information acquisition fun by converting elements of on-boarding into a competitive game with instant feedback. This can help to keep the attention of new employees.

- Rackspace populate their initial four-day on-boarding event with games, skits, costumes, thumping music, and a limbo bar.
- Bazaarvoice sends incoming employees on a five day scavenger hunt designed to bring them up to speed on company culture and company jargon.

Manage information carefully. There's a lot for incomers to learn so create reference-type materials, checklists and other materials that new recruits can access after the on-boarding process. Provide the material in bite-sized chunks so it's not overwhelming.

Make sure your new employee has support. This is where you could introduce a mentor. The mentor will oversee the initial job-specific orientation and be the first point of contact for the new employee to answer questions and deal with concerns. This will help the new employee gain specific guidance from an individual who has expert knowledge of that job.

Over the course of the first month, you can begin to put the new employee's role into the context of the company as a whole. For example, if you produce items for sale, the employee can have an online training seminar that is based on the production of the item. Encourage him to understand how the item is made, why you use the methods you do, and how this relates to both their role and the customer. After a month of successful orientation, your new employee will be better able to grasp what his role is in the company and will be armed with the knowledge he needs to succeed.

Extend the On-boarding Process

Extending the length of on-boarding can have a dramatic impact on employee turnover because it provides more time for coaching, sharing information and answering questions.

- L'Oréal offers a two-year long comprehensive on-boarding process.
- Succeeding@IBM is a two-year on-line learning continuum that provides new recruits with information covering corporate values, strategy, tools, and the resources necessary to be successful.
- Facebook requires six weeks at their on-boarding 'boot camp'.
- Rackspace and Zappos offer a four-week long on-boarding programme.

On-boarding Checklist

- Think about what you can do to start a structured on-boarding process prior to the employee's first day.
- Don't delay the start of on-boarding until later on in the week or month.
- Offer a way of allowing new employees to ask questions without being embarrassed. Provide a list of FAQs and answers covering areas of concern for previous new recruits.
- Ensure that their manager is present and available on their first day of work.
- Limit first day administrative sign-ups, so you don't bore new employees to death.
- Arrange meetings with managers and key employees and ensure frequent opportunities for two-way communications and feedback sessions.
- Make sure that the provision of space, work tools and equipment is closely integrated with the on-boarding process.
- Facilitate the building of the new employee's internal network and the rapid building of relationships with his colleagues.
- Prioritise jobs and customise the on-boarding process for the jobs with the highest business impact.
- Don't just highlight company values, but also show actual examples of how your employees live those values.
- Measure the time to minimum productivity, the retention rates for new employees and the satisfaction of new employees.
- Develop a process for rapidly sharing best practices and new problems related to on-boarding.
- Assess the training needs of new employees and ensure that any training needed is available close to their start date.
- Develop the capability to do orientation remotely using the Intranet, social media and teleconferencing.

- Provide new employees with a glossary of acronyms, buzzwords and a 'who's who' list of key people.
- Provide a tool that will create an internal social structure, for example Yammer (www.yammer.com) with employee picture and profile gallery to make assimilation easier.
- Get some feedback. On-boarding can play a critical role in improving your recruiting processes. Start by surveying your new employees about the recruiting process that they have just completed. Ask them which factors caused them to say yes to your offer, and which parts of the recruiting process worked and which ones need to be improved.

Case Study On-boarding: Google

Joining a new organisation is exciting but can be a bit nerve-wracking. Imagine what it's like joining one of the most famous and dynamic companies on the planet - Google. Nooglers (new Googlers) may have quite a challenging time settling in. Google developed a process for on-boarding Nooglers that reduced a new employee's time from start to productivity by a full month - a 25% improvement.

The process is straightforward. Google's People Operations send a reminder alert email to the manager of a new recruit the Sunday before the new employee starts. The goal of this just-in-time reminder checklist is to prompt managers about the five small tasks that have proven to have the highest impact on the productivity of their new hire.

1. Have a role and responsibilities discussion with the new employee.
2. Match your new employee with a peer buddy.
3. Help your new employee build a social network.
4. Set up on-boarding check-ins once a month for your new employee's first six months.
5. Encourage open dialogue.

Each element of the checklist has some additional guidance to prompt the manager, including links to templates, reminders as to time scales and useful questions for the manager to ask. Nooglers were also given guidance to help them transition.

1. Ask questions, lots of questions!
2. Schedule regular one – to – ones with your manager.
3. Get to know your team.
4. Actively solicit feedback – don't wait for it!

5. Accept the challenge (i.e. take risks and don't be afraid to fail … other Googlers will support you).

Two weeks later they receive a follow up email reminding them of these actions.

It is such a simple process. Too simple? Former Google Senior Vice President of People Operations, Laszlo Bock, writes that far from offending managers they were grateful for the simplicity and user-friendliness of the checklist.

Case Study: Trainee HR Consultants

When I first changed my recruitment process to recruit non-HR people I knew that I was bringing reflectors into the business. They need structure, method and order. The crazed kaleidoscope of daily change in our office would scare the living daylights out of them unless I managed their expectations. If I wrote the sort of things we regularly hear into a soap opera you would rubbish it as being too ridiculous and unlikely. Welcome to my world.

I knew that after the first three months they would get used to it and find the dynamism exciting but bringing them in carefully was crucial to their comfort and happiness (and by extension mine). At the time I was the only trained consultant so I had even less time than usual. Taking on two trainees was a big ask, but essential. I very carefully structured their induction. I created a version of the 'Don't Panic!' handbook (inspired by 'Hitchhiker's Guide to the Galaxy'.)

I explained the modular training system, much of which is self-study to start with, and provided all the materials. To vary the training we had the weekly Tool Box Talks (which they all love to this day), monthly Lunchtime Learning, work-shadowing and group discussions. By the end of three months they were immersed, learning well and enjoying the rough and tumble of HR as much as I do.

Takeaways: Chapter 9 On-boarding

- The way you bring people into the business is just as important as recruiting the right talent. Use pre-boarding to engage new recruits.
- Stagger the information you want new employees to take in over a period of time.
- Start by introducing them to their immediate team, their manager and colleagues with whom they will work closely.

YOUR NOTES

Key Points by Chapter

Chapter 1 Employer Branding

- Does your employer brand say the right things about your business?
- Work with your employees to fix anything about your employer brand that you don't like.
- Make sure your employer brand message is clearly and consistently communicated internally and externally.
- Keep monitoring and refreshing your brand.

Chapter 2 Where to Find Talent

- Keep the recruitment process continuously switched on.
- Look proactively at all the possible sources of good quality candidates.
- Measure the success of your recruitment process.
- Investigate growing the skills and experience you need by training raw talent.

Chapter 3 Benefits

- List and sell the benefits of working in your SME.

- Ask your team about the add-on benefits they want.
- Investigate creative ways of providing benefits at low cost.

Chapter 4 The Ideal Employee

- Be absolutely clear about whom you want to recruit.
- Create an ideal employee scorecard.
- Identify competencies, skills and attributes carefully.
- Consider cultural fit to ensure that a new recruit will mesh with the existing team.

Chapter 5 Attracting Talented Candidates

- Push the five interest buttons.
- Target your campaigns where your ideal candidates go.
- Take inspiration from creative recruitment campaigns.
- Consider making a recruitment video.
- Actively build a referral programme.
- Measure outcomes.

Chapter 6 Assess Applications Effectively

- Devise an efficient data collection process.
- Use structured interviews which question and allow you to probe into the candidate's competence.
- Use work-related testing to capture and assess relevant data.
- Use technology to streamline your process.
- Treat all candidates courteously, whether they have been successful or unsuccessful.

Chapter 7 Different Talent Pools

- Be aware of the different requirements for managing different generations of employees and manage accordingly.
- Communicate effectively and make your message available in multiple formats.
- Encourage mentoring and allow them to educate each other.
- Monitor all groups.
- Consider compensation and benefits to satisfy the needs of each group.

Chapter 8 Recruitment Case Studies

- The HR Consultant.
- The TrustMark CEO.
- The Sales Representative.
- The Barber.

Chapter 9 On-boarding

- The way you bring people into the business is just as important as recruiting the right talent.
- Use pre-boarding to engage new recruits.
- Stagger the information you want new employees to take in over a period of time.
- Start by introducing them to their immediate team, their manager and colleagues with whom they will work closely.

Further Reading and Resources

Further Reading

Good to Great - Jim Collins ISBN: 0201566620996
The Talent Magnet - Richard Evans ISBN: 9781535120593
Social Media Recruitment: How to Successfully Integrate Social Media into Recruitment Strategy - Andy Headworth ISBN: 9780749473709
Work Rules! Insights From Inside Google That Will Transform How You Live and Lead - Laszlo Bock ISBN: 9781444792362
Who: The A Method for Hiring - Geoff Smart and Randy Street ISBN 9780345504197
Y'd Awake:Understanding and Managing Generation Y – Zuza Scherer – Kindle
Mindset: The New Psychology of Success – Carol S Dweck ISBN-10: 0345472322

Free Download

How to Get Top Marks in … Recruiting the Right Person – Kate Russell ISBN 978-1-909324-08-4
To download your free recruitment e-book visit the Russell HR website and go to the HR Bar. https://russellhrconsulting.co.uk/shop/employment-e-books/. Click on 'buy now' and add this promotion code: DR5AMT5AM.

Resources

Apprenticeships
https://www.gov.uk/apprenticeships-guide
www.apprenticemakers.org
www.apprenticeships.org.uk
www.worldskillsuk.apprenticeships.org.uk

Ex-military Personnel
https://www.ctp.org.uk/employers
www.forcesrecruitment.co.uk
www.demobjob.co.uk
www.civvystreet.org

HR Zone	http://www.hrzone.com/
National Centre for	
Universities and Business	http://www.ncub.co.uk/
Erasmus International Internships	https://erasmusintern.org/
Recruiting ex-offenders	http://cleansheet.org.uk/
	http://recruit.unlock.org.uk/
Useful structured questions	www.va/gov/pbi/questions.asp
Internal social and	
network information	https://www.yammer.com/
Website traffic analytics	Google Analytics
	www.SumoMe.com

Applicant Tracking Systems
Free or fairly cheap ATS
https://www.zoho.com/recruit/
https://www.peoplehr.com/
http://www.proven.com/
https://www.freelancer.co.uk/
https://www.ziprecruiter.com/

https://www.smartrecruiters.com/

List of ATS products.
http://www.capterra.com/applicant-tracking-software/

Niche Job Boards

Aerospace and Aviation Job Boards

AerospaceJobs.co.uk
Britishaviationjobs.co.uk
Just4aviation.net
Onlineaviationjobs.com

Admin Job Boards

AdminJobsNetwork.co.uk
Helpdeskjobs.co.uk
Officerecruit.com
PAjobsboard.co.uk
Receptionistjobsonline.co.uk
Secrecruit.co.uk

Construction Job Boards

ArchitectureJobs.co.uk
Architectsjobs.co.uk
BuildingServicesJobs.co.uk
ConstructionJobsNetwork.co.uk
Constructor.co.uk
Justconstruction.net
Recruitconstruction.com
Surveyingjobsvault.co.uk

Catering Job Boards

Cateringjobsboard.co.uk
Incatering.co.uk

Charity and Non Profit Job Boards

britishcharityjobs.co.uk
charityjobsboard.co.uk

Education Job Boards

Britishchildcarejobs.co.uk
Education-Jobs.co.uk
Educationjobsboard.co.uk
e4s.co.uk
TeachingJobsNetwork.co.uk
TeachNetwork.co.uk

Engineering Job Boards

CADjobs.co.uk
Electronicsjobs.co.uk
Electricaljobsboard.co.uk
EngineeringJobsNetwork.co.uk
Engineerboard.co.uk
EngineeringJobs.co.uk
Engineeringjobsnow.co.uk

Justengineers.net
Productionbase.co.uk

Finance Job Boards

Accjobs.com
AccountingJobsNetwork.co.uk
Accountancyjobsboard.co.uk
Myaccountancyjobs.com
Bankingjobsuk.co.uk
Bankingjobs.co.uk
Euromoneyiijobs.com
FinanceJobs.co.uk
FinanceJobsNetwork.co.uk

HR Job Boards

Inhr.co.uk
HRJobsNetwork.co.uk
HumanResourcesJobs.co.uk

IT Job Boards

BCSrecruit.com
Developerjobs.co.uk
Itjobsvault.co.uk
ITWebJobs.co.uk
ITJobsNetwork.co.uk
ITContractor.com
PurelyIT.co.uk
TopITconsultant.co.uk

Leisure / Hospitality Job Boards

LeisureVacancies.co.uk
Leisurejobsnow.co.uk
Traveljobs.co.uk

Marketing Job Boards

Marketingjobboard.co.uk
MarketingJobsNetwork.co.uk
Marketingjobsnow.co.uk

Medical / Scientific Job Boards

eMedcareers.co.uk
HealthcareJobsNetwork.co.uk
NursingJobsNetwork.co.uk
ScientificJobsNetwork.co.uk
Scientificjobsboard.co.uk

Retail Job Boards

Fashionjobsboard.co.uk
Highstreetcareers.co.uk
Inretail.co.uk
JobsRetail.co.uk
Retailjobsboard.co.uk
Storemanagerjobsnow.co.uk

Sales and Customer Service Job Boards

Instituteofcustomerservicejobs.com

SalesJobs.co.uk
SalesJobsNetwork.co.uk
Salesjobsvault.co.uk
SalesVacancies.com
Seniorsalesjobs.co.uk

Transport Job Boards

Britishautomotivejobs.co.uk
Careersinlogistics.co.uk
Drivingjobsboard.co.uk
Justrail.net
RailJobsNetwork.co.uk
TransportJobsNetwork.co.uk

Other Job Boards

AgriculturalJobsNetwork.co.uk
Careersinentertainment.co.uk
Careersinmedia.co.uk
MediaJobsNetwork.co.uk
Defencejobs.com
Justutilities.net

Legalprospects.com
Onlineinsurancejobs.co.uk
Oilcareers.com
ParttimeJobsNetwork.co.uk
Publicsectorjobs.net
Renewablescareers.com
Recjobs.co.uk
Telecomsjobsource.co.uk
Translationjobs.co.uk

Local Job Boards

Allinlondon.co.uk
Cityjobs.com
FuseJobs.co.uk
LocalRecruit.co.uk
London4jobs.co.uk
LondonNet.co.uk
OnlineSuffolk.co.uk
Scotland4Jobs.co.uk
Scotrecruit.com
Scotjobsnet.co.uk

Index